Study Strategies for Teens

A Teenage Guide to Exam Success and Getting Better Grades

Charlie Haven

Table of Contents

Introduction

High school is what kind of grows you into the person you are. I have great memories, good and bad, some learning experiences, and some that I'll take with me for the rest of my life. –Giancarlo Stanton

Dear Reader,

If you're like many teens, you're probably struggling to keep up with schoolwork and maintain good grades. You may feel like you're always working but still not achieving the desired results. You might be anxious about your future, worrying that your grades will determine your success in life. The good news is that you're not alone; proven techniques and strategies can help you, and you're in the right place to discover them.

I understand the pressure you're under. You may feel like you're constantly being pushed to perform by parents, teachers, and peers. You may feel like your grades define you and that your entire future depends on them. This can be overwhelming, and it's easy to feel like you're drowning in expectations. I have been where you are and know exactly how it feels to be in your position. The worry that comes with thinking about how to rack up your grades is very unsettling, and sometimes you wish it could all just stop. Believe it or not, no one is an overnight success; even people who look naturally brilliant have had to work hard, and everyone has setbacks and disappointments. Ask any successful or famous person, and they will have their own journey of personal setbacks, discouragements, and failures. What sets them apart is how they dealt with them, learned from their mistakes, and used their experiences, good and bad, to rocket fuel their future success.

I understand the need to be successful or get the best grades because that feels great. I also understand that it takes more than just desire and calls for extra work. By reading this book, you will learn the tools and strategies you need to succeed in school and beyond. You will learn how to set achievable goals, manage your time effectively, and develop habits that work for you. Learn how to study smarter and achieve your desired results without feeling stressed or overwhelmed by working around the clock.

Here are some of the benefits you'll gain from reading this book:

- Identifying your superpower and your "why."

- Understanding your learning style.

- How to create a winning team.

- How to work smarter, not harder, for better grades.

- Strategies for effective note-taking and organization.

- Techniques to improve your memory and retention of information.

- Strategies for managing exam day.

- How to deal with failure.

Life is a journey full of lifelong lessons, and because we are all imperfect, learning will never stop. Even at my age, I still learn new things that I had never thought of before in my life. The desire to keep learning was one of the reasons I set out to write this book because I want you to learn more about how to achieve success on your terms through the lessons and tips I put in here. As the proud parent of two teenagers, I'm passionate about helping teenagers succeed in all aspects of life and very aware of how challenging this stage of life can be. I see and feel their struggles to succeed with each day that goes by. This desire in them to be better people lured me into thinking about all the other teenagers going through the same situation, and the end result of my thinking encouraged me to write this book.

Throughout my life, I have always had a keen interest in education and learning. I spend most of my days learning ways to be a better individual, parent, partner, friend, or colleague. In this fast-paced world that keeps evolving, it's imperative that you're always updated and learning something new. I am particularly passionate about this book because I not only feel like I'm communicating with a teenager struggling with grades but also feel like I'm communicating with someone who desires to see themselves successful and improved throughout life.

This is not just another study guide; it's a comprehensive resource that will help you develop the skills and mindset you need to succeed in school and in life. Passing exams is not the end destination; it's a step on the journey, a step that, if you approach it in the right way, will equip you with skills, attitudes, and beliefs that will spur you on to future success in life. And that is why, in our final chapter, we talk about where you go after this. It's important to start thinking about what you want your life to be like after exams. It should not end with getting an A but also push you to get a lot more A's throughout your life—an A in career, family, friends, and relationships.

I invite you to join me on this journey of discovery and growth. Together, we can help you overcome the challenges you face and set you on a path to greater success. So, whether you're struggling to keep up with schoolwork or just looking for ways to improve your study habits, this book is for you. Let's get started!

Chapter 1:

There's Only One You

What makes you different or weird—that's your strength. –Meryl Streep

You're special. You're unique. You're a limited edition. There is only one of you. In this chapter, I want you to reflect on what makes you—what unique and amazing combination of strengths, desires, skills, and motivations you and only you possess? In other words, what is your superpower?

The Rules of the Game

One of the challenges of school is that it most readily rewards those who are good with words or numbers, but that is only part of the story. Take a moment and think about your best friends, your parents, or one of your brothers or sisters. What is it that they are brilliant at that makes them stand apart? Perhaps they're great at making people laugh, organizing social stuff, making things, or just getting things done. Let me demonstrate with some examples from my family. My husband is great with people. He is always making sure everyone is comfortable around him. He always turns his neck to ensure those around him are doing just fine. My daughter, on the other hand, is a huge stylist. She is always exerting her superpower on us, which can be incredibly helpful, I must say. Each morning or any other time we are at home, she observes each of us and adjusts what we put on. She can say, "That jacket does not look good with that shirt; let's try the other one." When we try out her suggestions, they are always on point. She never gets it wrong, and she loves doing it. Then there is my son, who is blessed with the superpower of enthusiasm. He is always super excited to work on anything he is assigned. He never complains about anything; he willingly and happily goes about his work. Looking at the different superpowers possessed by the people around me makes me appreciate that all of us out there are particularly good at something, and that is your superpower.

Superpowers

Let me ask you this: Have you ever felt like school only values one type of intelligence? Like, if you're not good at math, reading, or writing, then you're just not smart? I know I have. It can be frustrating and discouraging, especially if you have other talents or interests that don't fit neatly into those categories. These are your superpowers—the things that make you unique and different from others.

Why Does It Matter

You're probably wondering why knowing your superpower and your learning style matters. Thinking about your superpower and becoming more aware of it helps build confidence and self-belief, which are crucial to doing well at school. Self-belief keeps you going when things get tough, so the more you can cultivate it, the more resilient you will become. At your age, self-discovery is a very important thing that will enable you to understand your strengths and weaknesses. If you're to learn how to study smart, you must know what personal tools you can utilize to achieve that.

The majority of the students dislike the idea of studying and learning simply because they do not know what their learning style is. To exploit your learning style, you must be sure of what strengths you possess to guide you in doing this. For instance, let's say your superpower is to bring people together. How can you use this opportunity to learn and improve your grades? I mean, you could bring people together and tell them today it's about discussing the new concepts the teacher talked about. See, that's genius. First, you managed to bring people together, and now you're taking advantage of them to discuss group concepts you barely understood and may never understand if you decided to read on your own.

Another scenario: Let's say you're good at making people laugh, and your reputation is that you're a funny person to hang around because you have the jokes. How, then, can you use this superpower to benefit your grades at school? If you can make anyone laugh, then you can make friends with anyone. That's the first plus of your superpower. The most important part is: How will you utilize this friendship? You could make friends with some of the intelligent kids in your grade, invite them to watch an amazing comedy show over the weekend, and as you bond with them, you get to tell them about how hard it is for you to grasp concepts in class and request that they help you understand them better. As you can see, it's not rocket science. Your superpower may not be intelligence, but you can do a lot without being super intelligent by knowing your superpower.

What Is Your Superpower

Yes, I have been talking about superpowers here and there, but wait, just a minute. What is your superpower? Or what are your superpowers? It's easier to talk about how important it is to have superpowers, but it's another thing to know them and utilize them to be better at everything else in life. Before we go on, I want to let you know that no one is without a superpower. Everyone has a power within them that makes them different and special. You, too, have a superpower. Perhaps you just don't know it. But worry not; we will understand how to identify that superpower within you.

The thing about superpowers is that because they come naturally to us, we're often unaware of them; we're either not even conscious of them or don't seem to see them as special or unique. It's only when we take a step back and consider this that we realize that we have unique strengths to bring to the table.

According to Mehta (2021, para. 2), "If you want to learn to be exceptional at something, your best bet is to understand the unique areas of intelligence where you have an advantage and then build upon those strengths." Kumar Mehta, who is a Harvard psychologist, stressed that those unique areas of intelligence are your superpowers, and if you acknowledge them and understand them, you can definitely utilize them to boost them and cover up for the areas where you're deficient. You don't have to be good at everything. Perhaps you just have to be good at a few things and use that to stay ahead in life. In school, that matters a lot. For instance, if you understand better through one-on-one discussions with a friend, your best bet is to harness a stronger friendship. The idea is to find a positive spin around your strengths to feed your bigger goals. That is what smart people do to outcompete hard workers. Just like Jennifer Lopez said, "Don't push your weakness; play with your strength (Az Quotes, n.d.)."

Some models, exercises, and frameworks can guide you in identifying your strengths. Below are some of the models I found helpful in determining your superpower.

Strengths Spotting

The best way to identify your superpower is to ask people who know you best what they think your strengths are. This particular exercise is quite easy to execute. It's sometimes hard to utilize the predesigned models because they may not give you the most accurate results, but when you ask people who relate to, share with, and live with you, you're more likely to get an unbiased opinion of your strengths. By hearing from friends, family members, or teachers about what they see as your strengths, you can start to better understand yourself and how you can use your strengths to improve your grades and life in general. However, if the idea of asking people what your strengths are just makes you cringe, or you're looking for some validation or more clues, then there are some great models you can use.

The 4 Es Model

This is not a standardized model, but I love it because each time I have used it, it has provided positive results. This model identifies four activities that can help you discover your strengths: energy, enjoyment, excellence, and easiness. You can list activities that fit each category and then identify the activities that appear in more than one category. For example, if you excel at math (excellence) and enjoy solving puzzles (enjoyment), you may discover that you have a strength in problem-solving. Here is a list of activities you can include to get started—don't overthink it. Just brainstorm for 5–10 minutes: what gives me energy, what do I enjoy, what am I good at? (excellence), and what comes easily to me? Write them down. It could be as simple as reading a book, walking the dog, or designing invitations for a party; all will give clues about your strengths.

- running
- hiking
- yoga
- weightlifting
- reading
- public speaking
- leadership

- time management

- organization

- planning

- multitasking

These are some of the activities that you can categorize under the 4Es.

Passion Mapping

Passion Mapping is also a simplified visual exercise where you can map out your interests and passions in different areas, such as sports, hobbies, school subjects, or extracurricular activities. By identifying what you're passionate about, you can start to see where your natural strengths lie and how you can use those strengths to improve your academic performance or pursue a fulfilling career.

Here's a step-by-step guide on how to do it:

1. Take some time to reflect on your interests, values, and experiences. Consider the activities, topics, or causes that truly excite and inspire you. Consider the moments when you felt most alive, fulfilled, and engaged. Make a list of your interests and write down your thoughts.

2. Divide your passions into different categories based on the areas of your life that are important to you. Common categories include career, personal development, relationships, hobbies, health, and community involvement. Feel free to make your own categories based on your specific situation.

3. Brainstorm and expand: Within each category, brainstorm and expand on your passions. Write down specific interests, goals, or ideas related to each passion. At this point, don't worry about

filtering or organizing; the goal is to generate a comprehensive list of possibilities.

4. Connect your passions to specific goals or aspirations: Begin by connecting your passions to specific goals or aspirations within each category. Consider how your interests can be integrated into various aspects of your life. For example, if writing is one of your interests, you could link it to a goal of becoming a published author or starting a blog.

5. Visualization: Select a method for creating a visual representation of your passion map. This can be accomplished with a pen and paper, a whiteboard, sticky notes, or digital tools such as mind-mapping software or online diagramming platforms. Use the chosen medium to map out the connections between your passions and goals within each category.

6. Examine and improve: Take a step back and examine your passion map. Assess if it accurately reflects your passions, interests, and aspirations. Then, make any necessary adjustments or refinements to ensure it accurately represents your true self.

7. Use it as a guide: Once your passion map is complete, use it for decision-making and goal-setting. Refer to it when considering new opportunities or making choices in your personal or professional life. It can assist you in aligning your actions and decisions with what truly matters to you.

Take the Quiz

Quizzes are another great tool to use. Below is a simple quiz that you can use to identify your superpowers. Carefully go through it, and then use the analysis after tallying up your results to know where you belong.

1. When you're working on a school project, which of these activities do you enjoy the most?

A. Researching information and compiling data.

B. Organizing and planning out the project.

C. Creating visual aids, like diagrams or infographics.

D. Presenting the project to the class.

    2. Which strategies do you find most effective when you're studying for a test?

A. Taking detailed notes during class and reviewing them regularly.

B. Breaking down the material into smaller parts and studying one section at a time.

C. Drawing pictures or diagrams to help you remember the information.

D. Teaching the material to someone else, like a friend or family member.

    3. When you're working on a group project, which of these roles do you typically take on?

A. Researcher or fact-checker

B. Organizer or project manager

C. Designer or visual artist

D. Presenter or spokesperson

    4. When facing a difficult problem, which of these approaches do you usually take?

A. Gather as much information as possible before making a decision.

B. Break the problem down into smaller parts and tackle each part individually.

C. Visualize the problem and come up with a creative solution.

D. Brainstorm with others and consider different perspectives before making a decision.

    5.   When you're stressed or overwhelmed, which of these activities helps you relax and recharge?

A. Organizing or tidying up your space.

B. Exercising or going for a walk outside.

C. Doing something creative, like drawing or writing.

D. Talking to a friend or family member about your feelings.

Now tally up your results and compare them according to the criteria below.

Mostly A's: Your superpower might be research and analysis. You have a natural talent for gathering and synthesizing information, which can help you excel in classes that require research and critical thinking skills.

Mostly B's: Your superpower might be organization and planning. You have a natural talent for breaking down complex tasks and organizing them to make them more manageable, which can help you stay on top of your schoolwork.

Mostly C's: Your superpower might be creativity and design. You have a natural talent for visualizing and creating, which can help you excel in classes that require creative thinking, such as art or graphic design.

Mostly D's: Your superpowers might be communication and leadership. You have a natural talent for working with others and presenting your ideas in a clear and compelling way, which can help you excel in group projects and public speaking assignments.

Now take a step back and crystallize all your thinking into some simple, clear sentences. Fill in the blanks. My strengths are... (write down at least three). Once you've written them down, don't just file them away in a drawer; think about how to leverage those strengths to work smarter and achieve more. Are you good at getting along with people? Join a study discussion group. Are you good at drawing or making things? Make sure you build that into learning and studying (we'll talk more about learning styles and tools later). And if you're aware of your strengths, you can partner with others with different strengths and rocket fuel your success that way (more of that later). You've taken the first step—you're much more aware of where you get your energy from, what comes easily to you, and what you're great at—and that insight is powerful if you keep focused on it and allow it to guide your approach to study and to life.

In the following chapter, we will learn why it's important for you to set goals for yourself.

Chapter 2:

Find Your "Why"

You do not have to be great to start, but you must start to be great. –Zig Ziglar

Before embarking on any journey, it's always crucial to answer the question, "Why?" When we leave this question unanswered, we simply set ourselves up to go with what is convenient. My teacher in 11th grade used to pep-talk us quite often and emphasize that before you do anything, always ask yourself why. Why am I going to this party? Why am I missing class? Why am I saving my money? Why am I at school? She insisted that everything that happens in life—everything we do—has a reason, and that reason lies in the why.

If you took the liberty and courage to always ask yourself why before doing anything, you would realize that you're capable of making better decisions. However, we often just go with what we think is right, what others are doing, our instincts, or what we are told to do. This is the wrong way of living because, most times, we find ourselves back at square one because we have not answered the question of why.

In this chapter, we are going to answer why. Why am I at school? Why are my grades poor? Why do I want to improve my grades? Why am I studying so hard? Why am I reading this book? We shall also explore ways to find your "why" and the several benefits of finding your "why." Finally, we will discuss how to set SMART goals. If you're looking at improving your grades to answer your "why," you need to be able to set realistic and feasible goals.

What Is Your "Why"

We all have different reasons why we want to do better in life. Some people want to do better to prove a point to someone. Others want to do better because they are naturally competitive. Some people like to improve because they have set goals that they want to achieve. Some want to improve because they are told to improve. My reason for pushing myself to be better each day may not be the same reason you wake up at the same time as me. Similarly, this is what is happening in school. Almost everyone in your grade is working hard to get better grades than last time, but the reasons why they are pushing for better grades are quite different.

If you carried out a survey, you would be shocked by the "whys" of your peers. You will learn that some seek better grades to get into Harvard, Yale, or Stanford. It has always been their goal from an early age. You will also learn that some are struggling night and day because they want to be better than anyone else. The feeling of being above everyone else satisfies them, and they aim to fulfill that feeling. Others have sleepless nights because their parents or guardians have very high expectations for them, which have been made quite clear, including the consequences that will arise if they fail to meet the target. Finally, some of them want to improve in their exams to get good grades to enable them to go upstream. But the big question you should ask yourself here is, "Why do I seek better grades?" For me or someone else? Is it because I want to enroll in my dream course? Why?

It's crucial to find your "why" when improving your grades.

1. Start by reflecting on your current situation. Take some time to think about your current academic performance. Do you struggle with any subjects? How do you feel about your grades? Are you happy with your current level of achievement? By reflecting on your current situation, you can identify areas for improvement.

2. Think about your future goals. It's important to consider what you want to achieve in the future. For example, do you want to attend college? Pursue a specific career? Join a particular program or organization? Write down your goals and be specific. For example, if you want to attend college, consider what schools you want to apply to and what degree you want to pursue.

3. Consider the benefits of education. Education is an essential part of achieving your goals, but it's also important to understand why education is valuable. First, research the benefits of education, such as better job opportunities, higher earning potential, and personal growth. Then, think about how achieving good grades can help you achieve your future goals.

4. Identify external motivators: Are there any external factors motivating you to improve your grades? For example, do your parents or guardians expect you to get good grades? Are your friends doing well in school, and do you want to keep up? Consider these external factors and how they are impacting your motivation to improve.

5. Stay motivated at all times. Improving your grades can be challenging, but staying motivated is the key to success. Find ways to stay motivated, such as rewarding yourself for achieving milestones, surrounding yourself with supportive people, and reminding yourself of your "why" and the importance of education.

When you follow the steps above, you can find your "why." After reflecting on all of these points, fill in the end of this sentence:

I want to improve my grades, do better at math, and pass the exam because... (fill in the blank). And for this to grab, motivate, and keep you on track, the answer must focus on you. It can't be because your parents want you to do well or because you'll feel guilty if you fail; you have to find motivation for yourself.

And now that you have established your "why," your quest for improved grades gets a little easier because you know what you want and, most importantly, why you want it. The following section will discuss the benefits you will enjoy once you have found your "why."

Benefits of Finding Your "Why"

There are so many reasons why you need to find your "why." The benefits are numerous. It helps you stand ahead of the curve and know where you're going. J.F. Kennedy, the 35th US president, while delivering his speech at the Coliseum in North Carolina in 1960, said, "Effort and courage are not enough without purpose and direction" (John F. Kennedy Quote, n.d.) So many people out there admit that they wasted their strong years going after goals that did not resonate with their purpose and winning trophies that didn't matter to them, and by the time they realized they needed to wake up, it was pretty late. But you do not have to be like them. You won't be like them because once you have found your "why," it will be hard to stop. It's one thing to find your "why," and it's another to know the weight of your "why." You have to anticipate what you will get on your journey. You're choosing to study hard because you want to get into your dream course, but one thing you will notice is that the satisfaction of finding your "why" lies in the numerous benefits that come along.

An amazing story I always reflect on is that of Martin Luther King Jr. He was a leader and civil rights activist who led a purposeful life because he found his why and focused on fulfilling it. Martin Luther King Jr. came from a black community in Atlanta. Growing up, he experienced and witnessed abuse of human rights, and he made it his life's goal to fight for everyone's equal rights. He nationalized the struggle for civil rights, and at one point, the whole world was talking about him. Several years later, Martin is still recognized and celebrated for finding and fulfilling his why.

Purpose

What is your purpose? This is a tricky question, but if no one has ever told you before, let me be the one to tell you that your "why" answers the question of purpose. When you think critically, internalize all facts, and come up with a reason that answers your "why," you have tapped into your core purpose and aligned your "why" with your purpose. We all have our core purpose, which may differ from yours because we hold different aspirations in life.

To define "purpose," it's the underlying driving force that gives meaning and direction to our lives. Having a sense of purpose helps us set goals, prioritize our activities, and make decisions aligned with our deepest values and aspirations. When we have a clear sense of our purpose, we are more likely to feel fulfilled, engaged, and motivated in everything we do. Purpose can come in many forms, such as a passion for a particular cause, a desire to make a positive impact on the world, or a sense of personal fulfillment from achieving certain goals or milestones. Ultimately, purpose is a deeply personal and individual concept that varies from person to person.

By finding your "why," you definitely define your purpose, and there is no better discovery in life than the discovery of your purpose.

Focus

Focus is a very important attribute everyone should possess in life, especially as a student, because you cannot afford to lose any precious time. You need to utilize your time wisely for studying to have time for other goals in your life.

Finding your "why" is crucial and can help you stay more focused and motivated toward your goals. You can tune out distractions and stay on track with your priorities when you have a well-defined sense of purpose. Abraham Lincoln said, "Be sure you put your feet in the right place, then stand firm." (Popik, n.d.). Finding your "why" means putting your feet in the right place. This will allow you to make more meaningful progress toward your goals, which can be incredibly rewarding and motivating.

For instance, if your goal is to pass your exams well so that you can be admitted to Stanford to pursue your diploma in law, that is a well-defined goal. You have found your "why," so you have all the reasons to direct all your efforts and focus on satisfying your "why." As you focus on achieving the milestone, you develop the habit of focusing, which will benefit you for the rest of your life.

When you have a clear sense of your values and priorities, you'll be able to live a more authentic and fulfilling life that is aligned with your deepest beliefs and aspirations. This can help you find greater joy and satisfaction in everything you do and create a sense of inner peace and contentment that is hard to find in other ways.

Clarity and Confidence

Beyond helping you stay focused, finding your "why" also provides you with a sense of clarity and confidence that can be incredibly empowering. When you know why you're working hard and what you're trying to achieve, you'll be more motivated, engaged, and energized by the challenges you face. This can help you push through obstacles and setbacks and inspire you to take bold and decisive action toward your goals. Have you ever picked up your study materials, sat in a quiet place, and started reading, and after an hour, you paused and asked yourself, "But why am I reading; what is the end goal?" and after thinking for a couple of minutes, you failed to come up with something substantial? Now that is a lack of clarity, and it comes with not knowing why you're there in the first place. Yes, you want to get better grades, but what happens afterward? You need to be clear about the plan. When all is clear, you develop a high level of confidence. Imagine you're pushing through tough classes, lessons, and exams, knowing that when you pass, you will apply to MIT, get admitted, and pursue your dream. That is clarity, and it attracts confidence. You're not confident in your abilities to pass because you're not sure where this leads. You, therefore, need to identify your "why," attain clarity, and build confidence. You will thank me later.

Goal-Oriented

If you have ten reasons for achieving your goals, finding your "why" gives you ten more reasons why you need to go after those goals. Finding your "why" can help you become proactive in your approach to life. Rather than simply reacting to circumstances as they arise, you can take charge of your life and actively work toward the future you want to create. This can help you make more intentional decisions, take more calculated risks, and create more meaningful change in your life.

If you know the goal that you're aiming for, you will work toward it and do nothing short of it. Your desire to achieve it will transcend any force that may dare to steer you off. Your "why" is the kind of force that will keep you oriented in the right direction toward your goals. As a student, I understand you may have a lot of ambitions and dreams, and I need to let you know that now is the time to start directing efforts toward fulfilling those dreams. Remember that dreams are just dreams without effort. The best way to start on the journey toward the aspirations you hold is to know why you hold them and then channel efforts in that direction. Wherever you are right now, now is the right time and place to start. Yesterday is gone, tomorrow is not promised, and today is the moment.

Skill Development

At every stage of your life, you will learn something new—that is a fact! The journey through life is all about constant learning and development. Where you stand right now as you struggle to improve those grades, meet your academic demands, and fulfill expectations is where you need to find your "why."

Discovering your "why" can also help you develop important skills and qualities that are essential for success. By doing this, you develop greater self-awareness as well as the ability to set and pursue meaningful goals. It can also help you develop a growth mindset, which is essential for learning, adapting, and thriving in today's fast-paced world. All these simple things that you keep adding to your life, like sprinkles of chocolate on ice cream, will turn out to be the most important parts of your life as you grow.

You will look back on your life and this moment in particular, and you will be grateful that you chose to find your "why" and develop the necessary skills quite early. You learned how to set goals and also developed a growth mindset. And you will be proud that all those decisions led to where you will be standing then.

SMART Goals

One of the benefits of finding your "why" is the ability to set meaningful goals. It's important to have goals because, without them, we aim at nothing. Everything you do as a student should be goal-motivated. Goals give you the motivation to rise in the morning and attend classes, read your notes, and complete projects and assignments. This is because at the back of your mind, you know there is something you must achieve, a particular result you aspire for, or somewhere you must be after all the efforts you have put in. That is motivation. Goals can be short-term or long-term. It doesn't matter. What matters is having them and working toward achieving them. This brings fulfillment and satisfies your inner purpose.

Each time you do not work toward your goals, you leave them hanging out there, and one day, maybe in the evening of your life, all these failed goals will sit beside you, and you will remember a moment when you could have brought them to life, but by then it may be too late.

But why do you need to set goals? Is it even important? I'm just a student; why would I set goals? Perhaps you have thought that way at some point in your life. Now, I need you to make a commitment to yourself that you will never harbor such thoughts because one thing is true: if you want to achieve your true potential, you need to set goals.

Why You Need Goals

This part was not intended to be part of the book, but I felt it was important to remind you why you need to set goals in your life. There are so many reasons why you need to set goals, but I will share the five strongest reasons that I find to be very important.

1. Goals provide direction. When you set a goal, you know where you want to go and what you want to achieve. This sense of direction can help you stay focused and make decisions that support your academic success.

2. Goals create a roadmap. Once you have a goal in mind, you can break it down into smaller steps. This roadmap can help you stay organized and on track as you work toward your objective.

3. Goals promote accountability. Setting a goal can help you take ownership of your academic performance. By setting a goal, you're making a commitment to yourself to work toward a specific outcome. This sense of accountability can be a powerful motivator to keep pushing yourself.

4. Goals increase motivation. When you have a clear goal in mind, you're more likely to feel motivated to take action. Whether it's studying harder or participating more in class, having a goal can help you stay motivated and energized.

5. Goals help measure progress. When you set a goal, you can measure your progress over time. This can help you see how far you've come and give you a sense of accomplishment as you move closer to your goal.

Those are the five core reasons why you need to set goals for life. You need to see where you're going; you need motivation to get there; you need to account for your actions while heading there; and you also need to measure how far you have reached on your journey. Now that you know why you need to set goals, let's look at how you can set SMART goals.

How to Set SMART Goals

It's not all about setting goals. We can all possibly set goals, but what matters is what kind of goals you're setting. Your goals should be SMART. SMART is an acronym that stands for "Specific, Measurable, Achievable, Relevant, and Time-bound (Talerico, 2022)." By creating goals that meet these criteria, you can create a roadmap for success and stay motivated as you work toward your objectives.

Here's a breakdown of how you can create SMART goals:

Specific

When setting a goal, it's important to be as specific as possible. Instead of saying, "I want to improve my grades," try saying, "I want to raise my math grade from a C to a B." It's easier to work on a specific goal than a general one. First off, a general goal is always bulky, and it may seem scary. Secondly, it creates tendencies toward procrastination because there are so many other goals embedded in a general goal; therefore, you may always find yourself reluctant to start at all because there are so many goals. Therefore, I implore you to break down the goals into smaller, more specific goals that are easier to tackle.

Measurable

Your goal should be measurable, so you can track your progress and know when you've achieved it. For example, "I want to read for 30 minutes every night before bed" is measurable because you can track whether or not you're hitting that 30-minute mark each night. Having a measurable goal also creates a sense of motivation. Let's imagine that instead of setting a goal to read for 30 minutes every day, you set a goal to read until you're tired. That is hard to measure because there are many dynamics to consider when determining when one is tired. There is no standard scale for fatigue.

Achievable

Your goal should be challenging but also realistic. If you set a goal that's too difficult, you'll get discouraged and may give up. On the other hand, if it's too easy, you may not feel motivated. For example, if you've been getting Ds in a subject, aiming for an A in one semester might be unrealistic. However, aiming for a C+ or B- could be achievable. I strongly encourage dreaming big. Having goals that make people turn their heads when you mention them is a good thing, but you have to be honest with yourself. What beauty is there in setting goals you may never achieve just because you want to dream big? There is satisfaction in achieving the goals we set for ourselves because, from there, we draw more motivation to set other achievable goals. We get to higher levels by taking things step by step and not jumping. When you try to jump, you may fall back, which is always hard and painful.

Relevant

Your goal should be relevant to your overall objective. If your goal doesn't relate to your desired outcome, you'll likely lose motivation. For example, if your overall objective is to get into a good college, setting a goal to read more books in your favorite genre may not be relevant. However, setting a goal to improve your SAT score could be more relevant.

The relevance of your goals speaks a lot about your purpose. At different stages of life, you will develop the need to come up with goals. These goals will be relevant to where you stand at the moment. When you hold on long enough to goals that are irrelevant to your purpose, you may lose focus on the relevant ones.

Time-Bound

Your goal should have a specific timeframe. This will help you stay focused and motivated. For example, "I want to raise my math grade from a C to a B by the end of the semester" is time-bound. Time is a crucial aspect when trying to achieve anything. If we did not attach time limits to the goals we set for ourselves, we would possibly spend the biggest part of our lives pursuing one goal. You may hate to hear it, but you may not achieve all the goals you set for yourself. You may be stuck in the quest if you allocate all your time to this. Therefore, as you set your specific, measurable, achievable, and relevant goal, ensure it's time-bound.

An example of a SMART goal is: "I want to improve my biology grade from a B to an A by the end of the quarter by studying for 45 minutes every night and attending a study group twice a week."

Now that you understand more about what you uniquely bring to the world and why you want to succeed, next, we're going to look at the importance of self-belief.

Chapter 3:

Believe You Can

Whether you think you can or you think you can't, you're right. –Henry Ford

I bet most of us have seen one, while some of you have driven a Ford. Well, Henry Ford founded the Ford Motor Company, which is the company that enabled a motoring revolution. This quote by Henry Ford highlights the importance of our mindset and the impact it can have on our ability to achieve our goals. It suggests that our beliefs and attitudes about our own abilities can either enable or limit our success.

All of us use the light bulb, but do we know who invented the first light bulb? I'm certain most of us don't. He was called Thomas Edison. His teacher did not believe in him. He was often reminded that he did not have the capability to learn or understand anything. This did not make Thomas lose his desire to keep trying. He championed a growth mindset. As much as people did not believe in him, he possessed the courage to believe that his skills and intelligence would develop. He made 1000 bulb experiments, all of which failed, and his 1001st was a success. That is belief. That's a growth mindset.

If we believe we are capable and competent, we are more likely to approach challenges with a positive attitude and a determination to succeed. This positive mindset can help us overcome obstacles and persevere in the face of difficulties, leading us to achieve our goals.

On the other hand, if we believe that we are not capable or that we are likely to fail, we are more likely to approach challenges with a negative attitude and a lack of confidence. This negative mindset can hinder our progress and prevent us from reaching our full potential.

The highlight of this chapter is belief. It is not enough that you identify your "why." You also need to believe that you can achieve it. You need to have confidence that you will get those amazing grades. You need to be optimistic that you will enroll at your favorite college for your dream course. To have faith and confidence and also believe that you can achieve all your goals is all part of having a growth mindset. In this chapter we shall talk extensively about the growth mindset, why it is crucial to have one, how to nurture one, and also compare it to a fixed mindset. You will learn that what is holding you back is not your lack of potential but rather your fixed mindset. Henry Ford did not have a fixed mindset, so he went ahead and built a transformational company that kept growing through challenges. You can be like Henry. Treat yourself as the company he decided to build, and focus on building yourself. It all starts with believing. If you believe, why not? What Henry Ford demonstrated was a "growth mindset.

Growth Mindset

According to Dweck (2006), "A growth mindset is the belief that skills and intelligence can be improved with effort and persistence." "People with a growth mindset embrace challenges, stay resilient in the face of difficulties, learn from constructive criticism, and seek out inspiration in others' success." Carol Dweck is an American psychologist famous for her work on motivation and mindset. She was an author at Stanford and wrote a popular book, "Mindset." She spent most of her time teaching people to nurture growth mindsets.

Each one of us out here possesses a mindset. A mindset is simply a conglomerate of beliefs and attitudes responsible for how you approach situations in life. The difference in mindsets lies in growth or fixation. Some people are naturally disposed toward a growth mindset, while others veer more toward a fixed mindset, but neither state is static nor fixed, and awareness is the first step. When I say that you possess a growth mindset, it means that you believe that your skills and achievements can be improved through effort and persistence. On the contrary, if you have more of a fixed mindset, you're far less likely to believe that change and improvement are possible.

Why is it important that you have a growth mindset? As a student, this is an attribute you should never lack. Every now and then, you're faced with so many challenges, and if you're pessimistic and believe that your skills and intelligence to handle those challenges cannot improve over time, you're more likely to fail at your goals. However, if you're optimistic that the challenges before you are a chance to learn and improve your skills and intelligence, you're more likely to triumph over them.

So many famous people in the world have had to have a growth mindset in life to succeed, such as Michael Jordan, Steve Jobs, Oprah Winfrey, J.K. Rowling, Albert Einstein, and many more. All of these successful, accomplished people have been told they wouldn't succeed or that they weren't good enough at points along their journey; the difference is how they reacted to that criticism. Of all of these people, I always loop back to Oprah Winfrey. I have never stopped referencing her story when telling my daughters, her friends, or other people about the importance of having a growth mindset.

In 2003, Oprah Winfrey became the world's first black female billionaire on the Forbes annual list (Chilton, 2021). This is not the point of the story. It is what Oprah has gone through all her life to reach where she is. It has been challenges on challenges, trails on trails, and yet she never thought of giving up but kept going. She learned and developed through the challenges. Oprah knew how to play the game of winning in life; she focused on being different from others because she believed that to be able to make a difference, you must be different (Jay, 2022). From being abused as a child to later building an empire for herself and many others and dining with famous people, including presidents and royalty, Oprah fulfilled the standard of a growth mindset by never accepting the limiting beliefs other people tried to put on her. I'm not a lover of stories of happily ever after, but Oprah's story is that one, and yet I love it. It comes from a place of pain and agony at times, a walk through the jungle, and eventually a fitting and fulfilled end. There are many stories of several people who have endured life with a growth mindset to get where they are, and these should serve as inspiration to you that wherever you are and whatever you're going through, with a growth mindset, you can achieve anything and everything.

Growth Mindset Versus Fixed Mindset

According to Dweck (2006), success depends primarily on mindset and not on talents and abilities. This should show you how important it is to have a growth mindset because, with a fixed one, you will never achieve all you're capable of. The biggest difference between a growth mindset and a fixed mindset is one we have already discussed. We agreed that a growth mindset believes that through learning and persistence, you can boost your skills and achievements. We also discussed that a fixed mindset is static and self-limiting.

Additionally, a growth mindset allows us to look at challenges as opportunities to learn and grow. In contrast, a fixed mindset sees challenges as problems meant to stop us from developing and growing. Let us look at two students in the same class, say Larry and Pete. Larry and Pete failed their most recent history exam badly, and things did not look good. Both are feeling the heat of the situation because if they do not improve their grades, they'll most likely miss out on enrolling in their dream courses. Amidst this, there is a big difference between Larry and Pete. Larry recognizes that he did not perform well but believes he can do better and is focused on studying and engaging in a discussion to bounce back. On the contrary, Pete has decided that he's just not good at history and that there's no point in trying, and he believes that however much energy he channels into passing the retake, he will probably still fail.

Looking at that scenario, we have to appreciate what it means to have a growth mindset. Both students face the same situation; however, Larry views it as a chance to learn from it and perform better in the next set of exams. On the other hand, Pete is not convinced that anything will change much, even if he puts in all his effort. He views the challenge of improving his grades as a problem he cannot conquer.

The Perks of Self-Belief and a Growth Mindset

Many people will tell you they believe in you. Others may not believe in you. Whether they believe in you or not, it is all vanity if you do not believe in yourself. Do you know what you can accomplish if you believe in yourself? Quite a lot, my friend. Now and then, I tell my daughters before they set off for school that it is not enough that I believe in them and their abilities to elevate their grades and excel at school. They need to believe in themselves more than anyone else. I never get tired of telling them to believe in themselves because I know just how easy it is to stop believing in your abilities while in high school. A one-time drop in math from A to D can make you doubt if school is for you or if you will even ever make it to college. It is that tricky out there for any teenager. Self-belief is fragile, and anytime self-doubt can come in. It is against that background that I decided to include a discussion on the importance of self-belief. I want you to appreciate the power in believing in yourself, and maybe every day, you will remember to foster self-belief.

To add, we need to acknowledge the benefits of nurturing a growth mindset.

Unlocks Potential

Everyone has untapped potential within them that needs to be unlocked. Only when you believe in yourself can you unlock that potential. There is more to you than the tension, pressure, and fear you have regarding your grades. This is just another hill for you to climb and move on to the next stage of life. With great potential, you can do amazing things. It is with great potential that you can convert that C into a B in one semester. All you need to do is tap into that potential to unlock your superpower and conquer all your fears. It is only through self-belief that you can unlock your potential. When you believe there is a power within you that can get anything done, you can truly get anything done. Henry Ford would definitely be proud of you. Believe that you have the potential, and then unblock that potential.

With a growth mindset, you're more likely to develop a love of learning and a curiosity about the world around you. Instead of seeing school as a chore or a burden, you can see it as an opportunity to explore new ideas and expand your knowledge. This can help you develop a lifelong love of learning and a thirst for knowledge that can serve you well.

For example, imagine that you're struggling in English class. Instead of seeing this as a failure or a reflection of your inherent ability, you approach the subject with curiosity and a desire to learn more. You seek out new books and authors to read, participate in class discussions and activities, and take advantage of opportunities to improve your writing and critical thinking skills. Over time, you develop a love of literature and writing and may even consider pursuing a career in a related field.

Supports Perseverance

As you struggle with your grades, there are so many things you need to stay focused on, and one of the most crucial ones is perseverance. Lucky for you, perseverance comes with self-belief. Let's face it, improving your grades is not easy. Sometimes you feel so beaten down by the overwhelming task that you start thinking of giving up. You wonder whether it is worth the sleepless nights, the several hours in the library, or the pain of research and assignments.

The inner voice that keeps telling you not to give up and keep pushing is what self-belief is. As long as you believe, you persevere. I failed so many times in school. So many times, my grades sucked. I wanted to throw in the towel and call it quits. I was tempted to think that maybe there was something else I was destined for besides doing well at school. I hope I'm wrong, but I understand you have felt the same way. Sometimes your grades have made you second-guess yourself, but you always persevere because you believe you will overcome. With time, I stopped looking at setbacks as roadblocks thrown my way to stop me from passing my exams but instead started looking at them as opportunities for growth. Each time I got an unpleasant grade, I developed the will to improve it in the next set of exams. That is just how vital self-belief can be.

Builds Confidence

All my life, I have not seen a combination as great as self-belief and self-confidence. It is insanely impossible to have the former and lack the latter. Self-belief breeds self-confidence, and if there is anything you need to achieve those amazing grades, it is self-confidence.

Self-belief builds the confidence you need to win now and later in life because once you believe in yourself and your abilities, you're most likely to believe in your decisions and actions.

If you're struggling with grades, it's easy to start believing that you're not cut out for academic success. But by focusing on your strengths and setting achievable goals, you can start believing that you can improve. As you start to see progress, your confidence will grow, and you'll be more motivated to keep going.

For example, let's say you're struggling with math. You might start by identifying specific areas where you need improvement, such as algebra or geometry. Then, you could set a goal to improve your grade by a certain percentage within a set timeframe. As you work toward this goal, you'll start to see improvement, which will build your self-belief and your confidence in your ability to succeed.

Self-belief can build self-confidence by helping you believe in your ability to learn. When you approach challenges with a growth mindset, you believe that you can learn and improve over time. This can help you see setbacks as opportunities to learn and grow rather than as evidence of your limitations.

Let's say you received a poor grade on a history essay. Instead of giving up or feeling discouraged, you could approach the assignment with a growth mindset. You might ask your teacher for feedback on how to improve or look for resources online to help you better understand the material. By believing in your ability to learn and improve, you'll be more confident in your ability to tackle similar assignments in the future.

Builds Resilience

If you're struggling to improve your grades, building resilience is essential to overcoming challenges and achieving your academic goals. Self-belief is a key ingredient in building resilience because it helps you believe in yourself and your ability to overcome obstacles.

When you believe in your ability to learn from mistakes, setbacks become opportunities for growth and improvement. Instead of giving up or feeling discouraged, you'll be more likely to look for solutions and ways to improve. This resilience can help you bounce back from setbacks and keep moving forward.

Let's say you received a poor grade on a test. Instead of giving up, you might review the material and identify areas you need to improve. By believing in your ability to learn from mistakes, you'll be more likely to approach the next test with a growth mindset, ready to learn and improve.

When you believe in your ability to persevere, you're more likely to keep going even when things get tough. This resilience can help you overcome challenges and achieve your goals, even when the path forward is difficult.

For example: You struggle to balance schoolwork with other commitments, such as sports or a part-time job. By believing in your ability to persevere, you'll be more likely to find ways to manage your time effectively and prioritize your goals. You might talk to your teachers or guidance counselor about strategies for managing your workload or seek support from your family and friends. By believing in your ability to overcome challenges, you'll be more resilient and likely to succeed.

Self-belief can also help you build resilience by helping you believe in your ability to make progress, even when the path forward is unclear. When you believe in yourself and your abilities, you're more likely to take risks and try new things, even if they seem daunting at first.

Additionally, a growth mindset can bring about adaptability and flexibility by encouraging you to view challenges and setbacks as opportunities for learning and growth rather than as reflections of your abilities. This mindset allows you to approach obstacles with an open mind and a willingness to try new strategies rather than becoming discouraged and giving up.

For example: You struggle to improve your grades in a particular subject, such as math. With a growth mindset, you will view a poor grade on a math test as an opportunity to learn and grow. You might seek out help from your teacher, work with a tutor, or try new study strategies in order to improve your performance. You would be open to feedback and willing to try new approaches, even if they are initially uncomfortable or challenging.

Enhances Motivation and Positivity

At all times, you need to maintain a positive attitude toward school, your grades, and your struggles. Secondly, it is important that you stay motivated throughout. Motivation and positivity do not fall from space; they are inspired by your belief in your ability to succeed regardless of the weight of the challenge.

Perhaps you'll take your first set of exams in high school, and things are not going as well as you'd hoped. You now realize everything is hard, and grasping concepts is almost impossible. In such times, it is easier to give up than to keep trying. And all you need in such moments is motivation and positivity. The way to this is through believing in yourself. When you believe in yourself and your abilities, you foster a positive outlook on life, and you will start to see the good in every situation. This will always help you stay motivated and positive, even when things are challenging. What happens when you have these moments is to keep going and keep the faith that you can triumph over your hurdles and achieve the academic excellence you're striving for.

If you struggle for reasons to believe in yourself and your abilities, focus on these five benefits and read on to find out how to develop a growth mindset.

Developing a Growth Mindset

Developing a growth mindset is not easy. It is not a "tick the box and move on" thing; it is an ongoing process, an attitude of mind that we all need to encourage, embrace, and develop at school and in life. No one is a finished product, and everyone will falter at different points. But just like a muscle you develop and strengthen through regular exercise with weights at the gym, the more you train your mind and your response to be that of a growth mindset, the more this growth mindset "muscle" will strengthen and grow and be strong enough over time to withstand setbacks. The truth is, our growth mindsets also differ, but what matters is that when you have a growth mindset, you're determined to keep learning and developing. The academic challenges in 9th grade are not the same as those in 11th grade; therefore, to be able to overcome the challenges as they come, you need to develop a growth mindset. With this, you will no longer look at them as problems but as opportunities for you to work harder and achieve more. The important thing is to start. Below are some tips that will help you establish and develop a growth mindset, but persistence and consistency are non-negotiable.

It's important to start by embracing challenges and seeing them as opportunities to learn and grow. Take on difficult tasks, such as studying for a tough exam or writing a challenging essay. You can build confidence and improve your abilities by facing these challenges head-on. You need to harness a positive attitude amidst challenges. With this, you will foster a growth mindset step by step.

It's also crucial that you learn from your failures. We have all failed at certain points. I have failed at various times at various things, and so will you. Instead of feeling discouraged or defeated by a low grade or poor performance, use it to reflect on what went wrong and how you can do better next time. Believe in the power of effort and understand that hard work and dedication can lead to success, even if you don't feel naturally gifted in a particular subject. A fall from B to D in math should not deter you from seeking improvement. It should inspire motivation and more determination to enable you to bounce back.

Maintaining a positive attitude is key. Rather than focusing on what you can't do, focus on the possibilities and opportunities for growth and learning. And when you encounter obstacles or setbacks, don't give up! Persevere through them, and remember that challenges are opportunities to learn and grow. Usually, when we fail, we just think about the negative side, beat ourselves up, criticize our efforts, and become hopeless, which is a trait of being fixed, and that is not who we want to be. Even when things are tough, and you feel like there is only one string of hope left within, choose to stay positive. Wake up early, pack your study material, show up, and be ready to improve your grades.

Develop a habit of seeking feedback. Ask your teacher how they think you can improve. Ask your peers for their feedback so that you can understand your weak spots and work on them. It may feel difficult and clumsy, to begin with, but developing this habit will be incredibly powerful and, I'm sure, inspiring, as you will discover so many strengths you did not realize you had, as well as the areas you need to work on. We are all our own worst critics, and hearing the views of others will usually dial down our own inner critic and boost our belief that things can change.

Practical Tips to Develop Your Mindset

- **Emphasize the power of "yet"**: Be open to adopting a "not yet" attitude instead of a "can't do" attitude. For example, instead of saying, "I can't do this math problem," say, "I can't do this math problem yet." Plus, developing the habit of jumping in and having a go is a great habit to develop not just for school but for life

- **Embrace challenges**: Don't be afraid to try new things or take on difficult tasks. Even if you don't succeed at first, you can learn from your mistakes and grow as a result.

- **Reframe negative self-talk**: When you catch yourself thinking negative thoughts, try to reframe them in a more positive way. Instead of saying, "I can't do this," say, "I haven't figured it out yet, but I'm working on it."

- **Celebrate effort, not just talent**: Remember that success is not just about natural talent but also about hard work and effort. When you put in the effort and make progress, celebrate your accomplishments and recognize your hard work.

- **Learn from failure**: When you experience failure or setbacks, don't give up! Instead, reflect on what you can learn from the experience and how you can improve in the future.

- **Set goals**: Setting goals can help you stay motivated and focused on what you want to achieve. Make sure to set realistic goals that challenge you but are also achievable.

- **Engage in self-reflection**: Take time to reflect on your progress and what you have learned from your experiences. This can help you identify areas where you have grown and areas where you can still improve.

- **Surround yourself with growth-minded people**: Seek out people who embody a growth mindset, such as successful entrepreneurs, friends, athletes, or artists. Learn from their experiences and ask for advice when you need it.

Developing a growth mindset takes time and practice, but by adopting these habits and beliefs, you can overcome your academic challenges and achieve success in your studies. Remember, you have the power to improve your abilities and achieve anything you set your mind to with dedication, hard work, and the right mindset. There are additional ways you can develop a growth mindset, and one of them is through exercises. Here is a link to visit, it has exercises and assessments designed to foster a growth mindset.

https://positivepsychology.com/mindset-activities-tests/

You must believe you can achieve anything. However, it is also crucial to remember that no one becomes successful overnight. There is a need for extra effort; there are setbacks; you will make mistakes, and you will have to pull yourself up and keep going. Giving up on this journey is quite easy, so you must strap yourself in and be ready to move, learn, grow, develop, and achieve regardless of the tests, trials, and obstacles. You must understand that no one is a natural genius, and all successful people, you see, have setbacks and make mistakes. The difference is that they keep going.

For example, look at Dallas Mavericks owner Mark Cuban; he is living proof that we learn from failure. Before Mark founded his first company, Microsolutions, he had failed at several jobs (Taube, 2014). He barely managed to pay his bills. He said he had made bad decisions that led him into such a position, but he was determined to learn from them. He never gave up but kept pushing and trying repeatedly, and he mentioned that one important thing he learned about failing is that you can fail multiple times, but you just need to be right once, and you will have your breakthrough (Taube, 2014).

So, it does not matter how many times you have failed your history tests or your math essentials; all you need to do is get them right once, and that will be the force that propels you to greater grades.

So far, we've explored the importance of understanding your "why," setting effective goals, and developing a growth mindset to enable you to succeed. Next, we'll explore different learning styles so that you can identify the one that plays to your strengths and propels you toward greater success.

Chapter 4:

Meet Bob and Nancy

Every child has a different learning style and pace. Each child is unique, not only capable of learning but also capable of succeeding. –Robert John Meehan

Bob likes to debate ideas and discuss concepts with classmates and his teacher, and when he's struggling, his first instinct is to ask questions. Meanwhile, Nancy likes to learn from pictures and diagrams; her first instinct when stuck is to go back to the diagrams and figure out where she's gone wrong. They are demonstrating different learning styles.

Learning styles refer to how individuals prefer to process and retain new information. Understanding your learning style can help you optimize your learning experience and achieve your academic and professional goals more effectively.

There are several different learning styles, including visual, auditory, kinesthetic, and reading/writing. Each learning style has its own unique characteristics and can be beneficial in different situations. It is important to note that most individuals do not exclusively fit into one learning style category, and having a mix of preferences is common. By understanding your learning style, you can tailor your study habits to maximize your learning potential and improve your academic or professional performance.

In this chapter, we will explore the different learning styles and how you can determine your learning style so that you can develop and exploit it to improve your grades.

Visual Style

This learning style involves using visual aids to process and understand new information. Simply put, with the visual learning style, we learn by seeing what we are learning about. People with a visual learning style tend to learn best when seeing things, such as pictures, diagrams, videos, and other visual representations. They may have difficulty learning through auditory or kinesthetic means.

The foundation of visual learning is that when information is presented visually, people can process it more quickly. This is because our brains are designed to quickly and effectively process visual information. Visual aids can improve our ability to remember information, understand complex concepts, and make connections between ideas.

Visual learning is the most common form of learning, and it instinctively starts in childhood. You notice that, as babies, most of the things you did were not taught to you, but by seeing what others around you were doing, you copied and mimicked what they did. Throughout your life, you have been learning visually, and as long as you can see, you will continue to learn visually. It may not be your strongest learning style; it will always stick with you.

Visual learning can be useful in various subjects, including science, math, history, and literature. Under visual learning, there are several tools that we can utilize to enhance learning, such as:

- Diagrams and flowcharts: For subjects such as science, math, and engineering, diagrams and flowcharts can be incredibly helpful. They allow you to see the relationships between different system parts and how they interact.

- Videos: Watching educational videos can be a great way to learn new concepts and reinforce understanding. Many online resources, such as Khan Academy and Crash Course, offer free educational videos on various topics.

- Flashcards: Flashcards are a great way to memorize important details, such as vocabulary words or formulas. You can create your own flashcards or use online resources such as Quizlet.

- Mind Maps: Mind maps are a visual tool that can help you organize your thoughts and ideas. You can use them to brainstorm ideas for essays or to outline the structure of a presentation.

One of the benefits of visual learning is that it can be a more engaging and enjoyable way of learning. When we are presented with interesting and colorful visuals, it can make the learning experience more stimulating and memorable. This can be especially helpful for students who struggle with traditional teaching methods. Visual learners are good at solving puzzles, interpreting graphs, illustrations, and pictures. On top of this, they always have a special and unique view of the surroundings. The way other learners may look at a scenario is different from theirs. Additionally, visual learners throughout history have become the most creative people.

Picasso was one of the most famous and talented painters in the world. According to famous writer Bhatt (2022), "Picasso turned out to be an entire school of painting because of the exceptional vision and spatial intelligence he poured into his work." There are so many great people in history who were visual learners, and by utilizing their style, they came up with several inventions, namely Albert Einstein (think e=mc2), Leonardo da Vinci (artist/scientist/inventor), and Frank Lloyd Wright (architect), among others.

However, it's important to note that visual learning may not be the best approach for everyone. Some people may find it difficult to process information presented primarily visually and prefer other learning styles, such as auditory or kinesthetic. It's important to understand your own learning style and to use a variety of methods to learn and retain new information.

Auditory Style

Auditory learning is a learning style in which people learn best through listening and speaking. Auditory learners can use this learning style to become more successful by seeking opportunities to listen and speak. This involves attending lectures, participating in discussions, and engaging in debates. They may also benefit from listening to audio recordings of books or lectures and using text-to-speech software to convert written text into spoken words.

One famous example of an auditory learner is former US President Barack Obama. Obama has described himself as a "visual learner," but he has also spoken about the importance of listening and speaking in his learning and leadership styles. In his memoir, *A Promised Land*, Obama writes about how he would spend hours listening to the radio as a child and how this helped to shape his understanding of the world. He also writes about the importance of listening to others and seeking out different perspectives in order to make informed decisions (Obama, 2020).

In addition to Obama, there are many other famous people who have used auditory learning to become successful. For example, Winston Churchill, one of the most iconic leaders in British history, was known for his powerful oratory skills and ability to inspire others through his speeches. Maya Angelou, the acclaimed American author, and poet, was also a gifted public speaker who used her voice to champion civil rights and social justice.

In conclusion, auditory learning is a valuable learning style that can help people learn and retain information more effectively through listening and speaking. By seeking out opportunities to listen and speak, using audio recordings and text-to-speech software, and engaging in discussions and debates as an auditory learner, you can enhance your learning experience and achieve greater success in your academic and professional endeavors.

Read/Write Style

Read/write learning style is a learning preference in which individuals learn best through reading and writing. People using this learning style tend to process information more effectively when presented in written form. They often prefer to read textbooks, articles, and other written material to better understand the subject matter. Additionally, they tend to be skilled at taking notes, summarizing information, and writing essays or reports.

People who use the read/write learning style can use it to become more successful by developing their reading and writing skills. They can take detailed notes and create outlines to help them organize and retain information. They can also benefit from using reference materials such as dictionaries, thesauruses, and other resources to expand their vocabulary and deepen their understanding of the material. It is possible to possess two learning styles, but I strongly believe I'm more of a read/write learner. Right from childhood, I have always loved writing. Sometimes I wrote unconsciously because I recall times I would simply be seated somewhere, bored, and holding a pencil, and I found myself scribbling meaningless things on paper, but there I was writing. As I grew up, I became interested in reading stories, books, and novels.

Additionally, I could never grasp concepts as the teacher discussed them in real time. I always took time to read and summarize them, and that is why I would be able to understand and memorize them. My love for reading and writing shaped the way I express myself because as much as

I can verbally express myself, the best way I can is by writing down how I feel.

I guess a good number of us have read the Harry Potter series. These series were written by a famous author, J.K. Rowling. She discovered that reading and writing was the best way she could learn and improve was through reading and writing. She went ahead to utilize this style to achieve success throughout her life. Rowling has spoken about her love of reading and writing from a young age and how this helped shape her career as an author. She has also emphasized the importance of reading widely and developing a strong vocabulary, which she believes is essential for effective writing.

Besides Rowling, many other successful individuals have used the read/write learning style to achieve success. For example, Bill Gates, the co-founder of Microsoft and one of the richest individuals in the world, is known for his love of reading and has credited books with helping him develop his ideas and insights. Warren Buffet, the billionaire investor, is also a prolific reader and has spoken about the importance of reading in his life and career.

The read/write learning style is a valuable learning preference that can help individuals learn and retain information more effectively through reading and writing. By developing your reading and writing skills, using note-taking and outlining techniques, and reading widely to expand your knowledge, you can achieve greater success in your academic and professional endeavors.

Kinesthetic Style

Kinesthetic learning is a learning style in which individuals learn best through physical activities such as touching, manipulating, and exploring objects and engaging in movement and physical experiences. This learning style is also called "tactile learning" or "hands-on learning."

People who use kinesthetic learning can use this style to become more successful by incorporating physical experiences and movement into their learning process. They can benefit from role-playing, simulations, and experiments that allow them to use their hands and bodies to explore and learn. They may also benefit from taking frequent breaks to move around and engage in physical activities and using tools such as diagrams and videos to help them understand abstract concepts.

The greatest physicist of all time is a renowned man, Albert Einstein, who is understood to be one who benefited from the kinesthetic learning style. He started talking late, and because of this, he started school when he was a little older than other kids. Einstein struggled in traditional educational settings; he learned best through hands-on experimentation and exploration. Lucky for him, his parents ran an electrochemical factory, so he always experimented and learned more by using his hands. He became a teacher at different universities and conferences because of his great knowledge. He once remarked, "I never teach my pupils; I only attempt to provide the conditions in which they can learn." He believed that learning should be an active process, and he encouraged his students to engage in physical activities and experimentation to deepen their understanding of the material.

As a teenager, you may find it difficult to focus and stay engaged during long study sessions, especially if you're someone who learns best through physical experiences and movement. If you're a kinesthetic learner, there are several strategies you can use to improve your grades and become more successful in your studies.

One of the most effective ways to utilize the kinesthetic learning style is to engage in hands-on activities related to the material you're studying. For example, if you're studying biology, you may benefit from using models and diagrams to help you understand complex concepts such as cell structures and systems. You may also find it helpful to participate in labs and experiments that allow you to physically interact with the subject matter. I have a close friend of mine, Sarah. Sarah had always loved working with children and had a natural gift for connecting with them. Despite not having any formal training as a teacher, she had a deep passion for education and a strong desire to positively impact young lives.

One day, Sarah heard about a local elementary school that needed substitute teachers. Eager to share her knowledge and enthusiasm, she decided to try it. As she entered the classroom for the first time, she was nervous but determined to make a difference.

To her surprise, the students instantly gravitated toward her warm and engaging personality. She created a vibrant and inclusive learning environment where students felt safe to express themselves and ask questions. Sarah's teaching style was unconventional, but her creativity knew no bounds. She would bring everyday objects to illustrate complex concepts, making learning an exciting adventure. This story made me appreciate practical learning the most.

Another strategy for you is to incorporate movement and physical activity into your study routine. You may benefit from taking frequent breaks to move around and stretch, which can help you stay focused and engaged during long study sessions. You may also benefit from using a standing desk or exercise ball as a seating option, as this can help you stay alert and engaged while studying.

In addition to hands-on activities and movement, kinesthetic learners may benefit from using tools like flashcards and study guides. These can help you engage with the material through physical touch and manipulation and can help you better retain and recall information.

Discover Your Learning Style

Discovering your learning style is very important, and there are several ways you can explore this. However, through personal experience and trials with others, I have found that taking a quiz is the most effective way. Here is a short quiz that will allow you to determine your dominant learning style.

1. When you're trying to learn something new, which of the following methods do you find most effective?

    a) Watching a video tutorial.

    b) Listening to someone explain it to you.

    c) Reading about it in a book or online.

    d) Trying it out for yourself.

2. How do you prefer to take notes during class?

    a) Drawing diagrams or pictures.

    b) Recording the lecture and listening to it later.

    c) Writing detailed notes.

    d) Moving around and fidgeting with objects while listening.

3. When you're working on a project, which of the following approaches do you find most helpful?

    a) Creating a visual presentation or poster.

    b) Discussing the project with others.

c) Writing a detailed report or essay.

d) Building a physical model or prototype.

4. How do you prefer to study for a test?

    a. Watching educational videos or documentaries.

    b. Listening to recordings of lectures or notes.

    c. Reading through your notes and textbooks.

    d. Taking practice tests or quizzes.

5. When you're trying to remember something, what do you tend to do?

    a. Visualize an image or scene in your mind.

    b. Repeat it out loud to yourself.

    c. Write it down multiple times.

    d. Physically act it out or demonstrate it.

6. How do you prefer to express your ideas and thoughts?

    a. Through drawings, diagrams, or visual aids.

    b. Through discussions and conversations with others.

    c. Through writing and journaling.

    d. Through physical demonstrations or examples.

Scoring: For each question, choose the letter that best describes your preferred learning style.

1. Visual

2. Auditory

3. Read/write

4. Kinesthetic

Add up the total number of letters for each letter you choose. The letter with the highest total represents your dominant learning style.

Interpretation:

- If you chose mostly A's, you're a visual learner.

- If you chose mostly B's, you're an auditory learner.

- If you chose mostly C's, you're a read/write learner.

- If you chose mostly D's, you're a kinesthetic learner.

It is possible to blend two learning styles. Your dominant style might be kinesthetic, but you're also a visual learner. Balancing learning styles can be challenging, but it is possible to incorporate multiple styles into your learning process. For instance, you can combine reading with physical activity. Kinesthetic learners tend to learn best when they are moving. You can try reading while walking, bouncing on a yoga ball, or doing another physical activity that allows you to move while you learn.

You need to translate your learning style into action to effectively harness it. You may create a table identifying the different strategies for your learning style. An example of such a table would look like this:

Learning style	Best strategies:
Visual learning	Use diagrams, videos, images, and mind maps to help visualize concepts. Highlight key points and use color coding to organize information. Create flashcards with visuals.
Auditory learning	Record lectures or discussions and listen to them repeatedly. Use mnemonic devices, rhymes, and songs to help remember information. Discuss concepts with others and explain them out loud.
Read/Write learning	Take notes while reading or listening to lectures. Rewrite notes and summarize information in your own words. Make use of outlines and bullet points to organize information. Use flashcards or quizzes to reinforce learning.
Kinesthetic Learning	Use hands-on activities and experiments to reinforce learning. Take breaks often and move around during study sessions. Make use of physical objects like models to help understand concepts.

Now you know your "why," you're working on your growth mindset, you understand your learning style, and the extra icing on the cake is leveraging your superpower. Now's the time to bring this all together with some good planning and execution hacks.

Chapter 5:

Plan to Succeed

All you need is the plan, the roadmap, and the courage to press on to your destination. –Earl Nightingale

Plan! Plan! Plan!

Winston Churchill said that if you fail to plan, you're planning to fail. I do not know if I'm the one who gets scared by the thought of failure, but yes, that has been one of my biggest fears. I have made it my life's goal to always be ahead. In everything I do, I ensure that I'm a step ahead. Raghava KK, a multidisciplinary artist whose work is shown in galleries and museums, was named one of the most remarkable people in 2010. He said that instead of having a 5-year plan, you need a 200-year plan. He insisted that the projects you manage will exist for generations; therefore, your plan should keep that in mind (Feddes, 2013). We may not all be creating art that will last for generations, but the principle of long-term planning is sound.

Benefits of Planning

Planning is an incredibly effective tool for helping you stay on track and make progress toward your objectives.

Break down your goals into manageable steps and prioritize your time and resources. This can help you achieve a sense of purpose and direction and ultimately boost your confidence and self-esteem.

With a clear "why" and a growth mindset, as a high school teenager, you're more likely to stay focused on your goals. Knowing what you want to achieve and believing you can improve your abilities through effort and hard work gives you a sense of purpose and direction. Planning helps you break down your goals into manageable steps and prioritize your time and resources accordingly, allowing you to stay on track and avoid distractions.

When you clearly understand your learning style, you can capitalize on your strengths and find ways to work on your weaknesses. This self-awareness can boost your confidence, as people are more likely to succeed when they work in a way that suits their natural abilities. Additionally, planning helps you set realistic goals and track your progress, enhancing your sense of accomplishment and self-esteem.

As a teenager, you often face multiple demands on your time, from academic work to extracurricular activities and social events. Planning allows you to manage your time effectively and avoid the stress and overwhelm that can come with feeling like you don't have enough time. With a growth mindset, you can approach time management as a skill that can be improved with practice, and you can use your understanding of your learning style to find strategies that work for you.

When you have a growth mindset and understand your learning style, you can optimize your study habits and strategies to achieve better academic results. Planning enables you to schedule study sessions, review material regularly, and set realistic goals for assignments and exams. You can improve your grades and overall academic performance as you track your progress and adjust your approach as needed.

How to Plan

The most essential part of planning is creating goals, which is an important part of achieving success in any area of life, whether personal or professional. Goals help us clarify our aspirations, identify the steps required to achieve them and measure progress.

Here are some steps to create goals and milestones to help achieve them:

1. Define your long-term goal: First, identify your long-term goal, such as improving your math score from 50 to 70.

2. Break down the goal into milestones: Next, break down the long-term goal into smaller milestones or interim points. For example, you could aim to improve your score by five points each month for the next four months, leading to a score of 70.

3. Identify the steps required: Once you have defined your milestones, identify the steps required to achieve each one. For example, if you need to improve your math score on Pythagoras, probability, and word problems, you could identify specific resources and activities to help you learn these topics.

4. Determine what you need to learn: To achieve your milestones, you may need to learn new skills or acquire new knowledge. For example, you could use online resources, like Khan Academy or Coursera, to brush up on Pythagoras or probability and practice solving word problems.

5. Identify behaviors to demonstrate: To achieve your milestones, you will need to adopt new behaviors or habits. For example, you could commit to practicing math problems for at least 30 minutes each day or seeking help from a tutor or teacher when you get stuck.

6. Monitor progress: To ensure you're progressing toward your goals, it's important to track your progress regularly. You could use a journal, a planner, or a spreadsheet to keep track of your scores, time spent practicing, and any obstacles you encounter.

7. Celebrate success: Finally, celebrate your successes, no matter how small they may seem. Acknowledge your progress and use it as motivation to continue working toward your long-term goal.

Planning is crucial to success because it lets you clarify your goals, break them down into bite-sized goals, and prioritize them.

The Tactics

Planning to succeed requires harnessing tactics that align with your learning style. The goal is to utilize these tactics to achieve success. To get you started, I've suggested five tactics for each learning style—so whether you're a visual, auditory, read/write or kinesthetic learner, I've got you covered.

Tactics are specific methods or strategies to achieve a particular goal or objective. In learning, tactics are techniques or approaches to improve one's ability to acquire, process, and retain information. For example, using flashcards to memorize vocabulary is a tactic that can be used to improve language learning. Similarly, taking notes and organizing information in a structured way is a tactic that can help improve studying and retention. Tactics can be tailored to individual learning styles and preferences and adapted and refined to optimize learning outcomes.

Visual learners:

- Watch videos or tutorials related to the topic you want to learn.

- Use diagrams, mind maps, charts, or graphs to visualize information.

- Take notes with different colored pens or highlighters to help important information stand out.

- Create flashcards with images or diagrams to help you remember key concepts.

- Use educational software or interactive apps that provide visual aids.

Auditory learners:

- Participate in group discussions or debates about the topic you want to learn.

- Listen to podcasts, audiobooks, or lectures on the topic.

- Record lectures or discussions to review them later.

- Use mnemonic devices such as songs or rhymes to remember information.

- Explain the concepts you're learning to someone else or have someone explain them to you.

Reading/writing learners:

- Read articles, books, or online resources.

- Take detailed notes while reading and summarize information in your own words.

- Write outlines or bullet points to organize information.

- Write summaries or reflections about what you learned.

- Use quizzes or practice exercises to test your knowledge.

Kinesthetic learners:

- Use hands-on activities such as experiments or simulations to learn.

- Take breaks to move around or engage in physical activity.

- Use objects to represent concepts or ideas.

- Practice problem-solving by working through examples or scenarios.

- Use role-playing or acting to explore different perspectives.

Creating a Timeline

After identifying the top five tactics, the next step is to create a timeline to roll out these tactics. First, a timeline provides a sense of progress because, as you work through your timeline, you can assess your progress. Secondly, a timeline creates room for accountability, improves time management skills, and guides decision-making. Here is a sample of a 4-week timeline that can guide you in rolling out the tactics aligned with your learning style. You'll want to adjust the suggestions depending on your learning style and preferences, but this gives you an idea of the breadth of areas you can work on and include.

Week 1:

- Monday: Determine your learning style by taking an online quiz or reflecting on your past experiences.

- Tuesday: Research and gather resources that align with your learning style (videos, articles, apps, etc.).

- Wednesday: Create a personalized plan that incorporates tactics that align with your learning style.

- Thursday: Start implementing your plan by trying one or two tactics for the day.

- Friday: Reflect on your progress and adjust your plan as needed.

Week 2:

- Monday: Continue implementing tactics from week 1 and try adding in a new one.

- Tuesday: Schedule time in your calendar to work on your learning plan each day.

- Wednesday: Check in with a friend or accountability partner to discuss your progress and challenges.

- Thursday: Take a break and engage in a physical activity that aligns with your learning style (e.g., going for a walk while listening to an audiobook).

- Friday: Reflect on your progress and celebrate your achievements.

Week 3:

- Monday: Continue implementing tactics from weeks 1 and 2 and try adding in a new one.

- Tuesday: Use a flashcard app or create physical flashcards to practice memorization.

- Wednesday: Schedule a study group or discussion session to engage with others who have a similar learning style.

- Thursday: Incorporate mindfulness or meditation practices to help reduce stress and improve focus.

- Friday: Reflect on your progress and adjust your plan as needed.

Week 4:

- Monday: Continue implementing tactics from weeks 1–3 and try adding in a new one.

- Tuesday: Use educational software or interactive apps that provide visual aids.

- Wednesday: Experiment with different learning environments to see what works best for you (e.g., studying in a quiet space versus a more social environment).

- Thursday: Use a role-playing or acting exercise to explore different perspectives related to what you're learning.

- Friday: Reflect on your progress and celebrate your achievements.

By the end of this timeline, you should have a better understanding of your learning style and the tactics that work best for you. You can continue to refine and adjust your plan as needed to optimize your learning outcomes.

Creating Milestones

Milestones are identifiable junctures in time or indicators of advancement toward a target or aim. They help divide a larger objective into more manageable, measurable and achievable tasks or steps. With the help of milestones, you can monitor your progress toward your goal and, if necessary, change your actions or strategies. Milestones can also act as checkpoints or indicators of progress.

Creating milestones is essential and can be a bit tricky; however, the following tips can be very helpful in guiding you on how to come up with the milestones.

- After deciding on your overarching objective, divide it up into more manageable, smaller steps. Your goal should become closer as you reach each milestone.

- Each milestone should represent a distinct action or accomplishment that can be tracked. This will enable you to monitor your progress and make any necessary corrections.

- Determine realistic and feasible due dates or timelines for each milestone based on your schedule, available resources, and other obligations.

- Each milestone should be broken down into specific actions or tasks that must be completed in order to achieve it. You can maintain your focus and make sure you're moving forward steadily by doing this.

- Track your development toward each milestone and recognize your successes along the way. If you're running behind, change your strategy or, if necessary, get assistance.

- Keep in mind that your milestones are a guide, not a strict schedule. Be adaptable and change your plan as necessary to reflect your progress and any alterations in your circumstances.

Following those steps, you can come up with great milestones to ensure you're still on track.

Exemplar Template

Here is an example of a template with milestones that can guide how to pass a test, say a math midterm test.

Math Midterm Test Preparation Milestones Template

1. Objective: Get a B on the mid-term test for [math course name].

2. Milestones:

Milestone 1: Assess your knowledge. Take a diagnostic test or quiz to assess your current understanding of the material.

- Timeline: [date 1]

- Action steps: Complete a diagnostic test or quiz covering the material in the mid-term, and review your results to identify areas where you need improvement.

Milestone 2: Review and practice the basic concepts and formulas covered in the first half of the course.

- Timeline: [date 2]

- Action steps: Review notes and textbook for the first half of the course, practice basic concepts and formulas using sample problems, and create flashcards or study guides to help you memorize important information.

Milestone 3: Focus on problem areas: Identify and focus on problem areas by working through example problems and seeking help from a teacher or tutor.

- Timeline: [date 3]

- Action steps: Review your results from the diagnostic test, identify your weakest areas, and focus on those areas by working through example problems and seeking help from your teacher or tutor.

Milestone 4: Review and practice advanced concepts and formulas covered in the second half of the course.

- Timeline: [date 4]

- Action steps: Review the notes and textbook for the second half of the course, practice advanced concepts and formulas using sample problems, and create flashcards or study guides to help you memorize important information.

Milestone 5: Complete practice tests: Complete multiple practice tests and review your answers to identify areas that need further improvement.

- Timeline: [date 5]

- Action steps: Complete at least two practice tests covering all material on the mid-term, review your answers, and identify areas that need further improvement.

Milestone 6: Review all course materials, summarize key concepts, and create a study plan for the final week of preparation.

- Timeline: [date 6]

- Action steps: Review all course materials, summarize key concepts, and create a study plan for the final week of preparation that focuses on your weakest areas.

Milestone 7: Test Day: Take the midterm test confidently and focus.

- Timeline: [test date]

- Action steps: Arrive early, bring all necessary materials, and stay calm and focused during the test.

3. Evaluation: After each milestone, evaluate your progress toward getting a B on the mid-term test. Adjust your study plan or seek help if needed.

In conclusion, it is crucial to always plan, lay out your milestones, design strategies, and move on to implement them. In the next chapter, we will explore how to work smart.

Chapter 6:

Working Smarter

Give me six hours to cut down a tree, and I will spend the first four sharpening the axe. –Abraham Lincoln

The hidden secret behind planning is that it allows you to work smart and not hard. Without a plan, you're more likely to spend way more time executing a task - with planning; the job is easier and faster.

Working smart means using effective strategies and techniques to achieve your goals in the most efficient and productive way possible. It involves focusing on the most important tasks and using resources wisely, such as time, energy, and skills. On the other hand, working hard emphasizes putting in long hours and effort without necessarily achieving better results.

Here is a scenario contrasting working hard and working smart.

John makes the decision to study hard for the exam. He reads through his class notes, makes notes, and studies everything in the textbook. He devotes a significant amount of time each day to studying, sometimes studying late into the night. He studies most of the time in his free time because he is determined to succeed.

Working Smart: In contrast, John's friend Sarah chooses to approach her exam in a clever manner. She begins by listing the most crucial subjects and questions that will be asked on the test. She then concentrates her studies on those subjects. She supplements her understanding of the subject using online resources like study aids and videos. She also makes flashcards to help her remember important details; she regularly tests herself to see if she has mastered the subject.

Here is the kicker: It's not all about working harder. It's about leveraging your superpower, knowing your learning style, creating a realistic plan, and then building in smart tactics to make your study time work for you.

Focus on Your "Why"

In Chapter 2, we discussed the importance of and how to find your "why." To work smart, you need to focus on your "why" as it will help to accelerate progress as you go after success.

Understanding your purpose and the motivations behind your actions and objectives is essential to focusing on your "why." Even in the face of difficulties and setbacks, clearly understanding your "why" can keep you motivated and focused. It helps you make decisions consistent with your values and goals and gives your work direction and meaning.

Knowing your "why" can also assist you in setting priorities for your work and concentrating your efforts on the tasks that will have the biggest impact. Understanding your purpose and what you want to accomplish will help you identify the tasks that will get you there and get rid of the ones that aren't as important or urgent.

Focusing on your "why" entails having a clear understanding of the methods and approaches that will enable you to accomplish your objectives quickly and successfully. You can find the most effective methods to complete tasks, streamline your workflow, and boost productivity by concentrating on your "why."

If your goal is to pass your finals and roll into your dream college, all strategies and techniques should be aimed at achieving the goal. The milestones in your design should be the ultimate guide to keeping you on track. That is what smart people do: they channel all their focus on the main goal.

Eat the Frog

According to Eat That Frog, a book written by Tracy (2013, p. 89), "It's important to start your day by doing the most hard or challenging task" This builds momentum and helps prevent procrastination and the most difficult tasks simply being bumped to the next day or week.

The truth is, there are not enough hours around the clock to get everything done; therefore, it is a no-brainer to kick off with the task you consider to be the most challenging and the most important.

Let's imagine a scenario where you have five goals to accomplish today. It is important to eat the frog first because once you successfully finish the hardest task, the rest will come to you with a little more ease. The list below contains five distinctive tasks that you would have to accomplish, and they are organized in the order of the most challenging to the least challenging.

1. Research and write a 5-page essay on a difficult topic assigned by your teacher.

2. Practice a difficult musical piece for an upcoming audition or performance.

3. Study for a challenging final exam in a difficult subject, such as Advanced Placement Calculus or Chemistry.

4. Complete a complex math problem set that requires critical thinking and problem-solving skills.

5. Clean and organize your room or living space, which may be a less challenging task but still requires focus and effort.

Looking at those five tasks, writing a 5-page essay is the most challenging compared to the rest. When you start your day by writing a 5-page essay, completing a complex math problem will be a little easier. On the other hand, if you start with cleaning your room, then move on to studying for the final exam in a difficult subject, by the time you start on the 5-page essay, you will probably be worn out and tired. This will lure you into procrastinating and postponing the assignment. You may have worked hard throughout the day, but you are not smart. Therefore, as you organize your goals and milestones, ensure that, when it comes to execution, you eat the frog first.

Miracle Morning

How you start the day is crucial to how the day will play out. Hal Elrod, the author of the international bestseller *Miracle Morning*, spent a long time looking into how successful people started their day. He found that some started with exercise, others with meditation, and others with writing in a diary. He started thinking about what would happen if you combined these habits into a morning routine—leveraging the power of these positive habits. He called this "the miracle morning." He called the practices the "SAVERS"—a contraction for Silence, Affirmations, Visualization, Exercise, Reading, and Scribing (Elrod, 2017).

Here's a brief overview of each of the SAVERS:

- Silence: This involves taking some time to sit quietly and clear your mind, whether through meditation, prayer, or simply focusing on your breath. In this era, we do not appreciate the gift of silence anymore. People wake up to TikTok, Snapchat, or Instagram stories. Others rush out of bed like they have been at war. However, it is crucial to set aside about five minutes to meditate or just sit quietly and reflect on how your day will go.

- Affirmations: These are positive statements focused on specific goals that are important to you. Hal Elrod suggests using sentences like "I am just as worthy, deserving, and capable of (fill in your goal) as any other person on earth, and I will prove that today with my actions." Or "I am committed to (fill in your goal) because of the impact it will have on my life, and today I will do (add in action) to move me toward this goal.

- Visualization: This is where you take each affirmation in turn and visualize what that outcome will look like and—equally importantly—visualize the activity you will do that day to keep you on track for that goal. Visualization is about creating an optimum emotional experience that will encourage you to do that next step that day.

- Exercise: Physical activity can help improve your mood, energy levels, and overall health. Once you start the day with a few pushups, situps, or stretches, you will feel energized throughout.

- Reading: Devoting some time each morning to reading can help expand your knowledge and inspire you. Read books outside the scope of school. Consider self-help or financial development books. They open your mind to a bigger picture.

- Scribing: This involves writing in a journal or diary, which can help you clarify your thoughts, process your emotions, and set goals for the day ahead.

Hal Elrod suggests that by practicing these "SAVERS" each morning, you can improve your focus, increase your productivity, and achieve your goals more effectively. Taking an hour each morning (10 minutes per saver) can be very powerful. If that feels unreachable, try just 5 minutes, so 30 minutes. The book also provides tips and strategies for overcoming obstacles and sticking with the Miracle Morning routine. He emphasizes that with focus, effort, and consistency, your success is inevitable; it's only a matter of time, and the SAVERS help us all "override the fear of failure with a belief we will succeed" (Elrod, 2017). So to work smart, aim to incorporate the "SAVERS" into your life each morning so you're ahead of the curve.

Marginal Gains

The philosophy of marginal gains emphasizes the idea that small improvements, when added together, can result in significant overall improvements. Dave Brailsford, former performance director for British Cycling and current general manager of Team INEOS, popularized the concept, which has since been widely applied in fields ranging from sports to business to personal development. Brailsford's philosophy was focused on the "aggregation of marginal gains," the idea that if you made small improvements in many areas, the overall impact would be transformational. When he took over, the team had the dubious honor of having only won one gold medal at the Olympics since 1908. So he went to work; he looked at everything from the kit the team wore to the design of the bikes, the food they ate, and the training regime, and he was right; these small 1% gains in many areas led to a radical impact overall. Five years after he took over, British cycling scooped 60% of the cycling medals at the Beijing Olympics (Bokhari, 2020).

Our biggest problem is that we want instant results. We think success comes overnight as if it were magic, yet if we direct our efforts toward small, incremental steps, we will achieve more in the long run.

Smart people assess the important areas in their journey, then set a goal to improve each area by small margins each day. For instance, Jenny is a high school sophomore who wants to improve her academic performance. She has struggled with time management and study habits, and her grades have suffered. Jenny decides to apply the concept of marginal gains to her academic work to work smart and improve her grades.

First, Jenny breaks down her goal of improving her grades into smaller, more manageable components. She identifies three areas for improvement: time management, study habits, and understanding specific subjects.

For time management, Jenny set aside a specific time each day for homework and studying. She breaks her assignments into smaller tasks and sets specific goals for each study session. She also sets aside time weekly to review her progress and adjust her study schedule.

For study habits, Jenny focuses on small improvements such as minimizing distractions, taking regular breaks, and reviewing her notes regularly. She also seeks help from her teachers and tutors when needed and works to develop a more active and engaged approach to learning.

To understand specific subjects, Jenny focuses on small improvements such as reading her textbooks more thoroughly, taking more detailed notes, and seeking clarification on areas of confusion. She also sets aside time each week to review previous material and ensure a solid understanding of the concepts covered in class.

Jenny tracks her progress over time, keeping track of her grades, study habits, and time management. She celebrates small successes along the way, such as improving her grades on a specific assignment or consistently meeting her study goals for a week or month. Over time, Jenny's small improvements add up, and she sees a significant overall improvement in her academic performance.

The Extras

Above the primary strategies of working smart, there are extra strategies you can include in your day to give you an extra edge.

Designated Study Area

First, having a dedicated study area can help you establish a routine and give your study sessions some structure. Your brain receives a signal when you have a specific area set aside for studying that it is time to concentrate and be effective. You'll be able to focus better and get into the right frame of mind for studying.

Keeping your study area neat and organized can also aid in lowering distractions and enhancing focus. When your workspace is cluttered and disorganized, it can be difficult to focus on your work, and you may become distracted by unrelated items or tasks. Keeping your study area neat and organized can reduce distractions and create a more conducive learning environment.

Having a well-organized study area can also help you be more efficient. You can avoid wasting time looking for materials and becoming distracted by unrelated tasks if you have all the materials you need nearby and know where everything is. This can assist you in remaining focused and making the most of your study time.

Last but not least, setting up a dedicated study area that is welcoming and helpful for learning can make studying more enjoyable for you. You might discover that you enjoy learning and remembering information more than you would in a less conducive environment if you have a room that is well-lit, cozy, and free of distractions.

Study in Short Bursts

When it comes to studying, you might think that spending long hours cramming in as much information as possible is the best way to go. However, the truth is that studying in short bursts is a much more effective way to learn and retain information.

Studying in short bursts, typically 25–30 minutes long, is known as the Pomodoro technique. Francis Cirillo, a university student, created this method due to a study problem. It was hard for him to focus, like the majority of us. I mean, one minute you're reading, and the next, your mind is all over the place. Francis dedicated a few uninterrupted minutes to his work while taking short breaks and then resumed (Scroggs, 2022). The idea behind this technique is that short, focused bursts of studying are more effective than long hours of cramming.

You can maintain a higher level of focus and concentration when you study in short bursts. You can better stay on task and avoid distractions by segmenting your study sessions into smaller, more manageable chunks.

To add to this, studying in short bursts is more effective for memory retention than cramming for long periods. Taking breaks between study sessions allows your brain to process the material yearned for, enhancing long-term retention.

You're more likely to be time-effective and productive when you study in short sessions. It can be a motivator to stay focused and prevent procrastination when you're aware of the time constraints on your study time.

Long study sessions can also be exhausting and cause burnout. By allowing you to take frequent breaks to recharge your batteries and return to your studies revitalized and energized, studying in short bursts can help you avoid burnout.

Eat Well

Eating a nutritious diet is not only essential for your overall health but can also have a significant impact on your ability to work smarter. The brain needs proper nourishment to work effectively. Eating in the right way will mean you'll have good energy levels, a balanced mood, a sharper mind, and be able to sleep better - who wouldn't want that? So what is the right way?

The Mediterranean diet has been shown consistently in multiple studies to provide all these benefits and more (Guasch-Ferré & Willett, 2021). It focuses on a wholefood, plant-based diet high in complex carbohydrates, fiber, fruits, and vegetables and low in refined sugar, red meat, saturated fat, and foods with additives and preservatives.

Eating the Mediterranean way doesn't have to be complicated; simple is often better. A day eating this way could look like this:

Breakfast:

Eggs/avocado on whole grain toast for breakfast.

Porridge oats with fresh berries, Greek yogurt, and a sprinkle of seeds.

Lunch:

Salad or whole grain sandwich with grilled chicken/salmon.

Bean or lentil soup with oodles of vegetables.

Dinner:

Grilled fish/chicken with vegetables and brown rice.

Seafood stir fry with vegetables and noodles.

Avoid sugary drinks, snacks, and ultra-processed foods such as chips, sweets, and biscuits - they will spike your blood sugar (leading to the inevitable sugar crash later), affecting your mood and your focus. And make sure you're eating oily fish such as salmon, mackerel, or sardines two to three times a week (crucial for omega 3's, which are fats the brain needs to work well).

Finally, when you eat is also important. Eating a great breakfast sets you up for the day (remember, it has to be a good breakfast, such as those eggs or porridge oats) and will help you keep your blood sugar and, therefore, your energy and mood stable throughout the day. Equally, try to avoid eating late into the evening because your body will still digest the food when you want to sleep, which won't help you get good rest.

When it comes to diet—the advice is simple, consistent execution is where most people come unstuck, so recognize the importance of food, try and keep consistent, and follow the 80/20 rule—eat well for 80% of the time and don't expect perfection. If, when you read this section, you think, "Wow, I need a radical overhaul of my diet,"slow and steady generally wins the race. You may be one of the few who can throw everything up in the air, create a whole new regime overnight, and make it stick. But for most people, most of the time, slow and steady wins the race most of the time. Making small, incremental changes over time is a great way to radically change your lifestyle (remember the power of marginal gains). In six months, you'll look back and realize how far you have come and how much your tastebuds and appetites have changed.

In summary, smart work beats hard work by a mile. You cannot spend the whole day reading and cramming concepts; instead, utilize these hacks and start to work smart. You can utilize three hours or less out of your day studying smart, and you will benefit more than someone who uses the entire day working hard without smart strategies.

Working smart is crucial, but this is not a solo sport. You need to create a winning team. A winning team is an essential support system that you will need to achieve your goals.

Chapter 7:

Create a Winning Team

Be strong, be fearless, and be beautiful. And believe that anything is possible when you have the right people there to support you. –Misty Copeland

Part of learning to succeed is learning that studying for success is a team sport, not a solo act. I have learned so many lessons, and one of the most valuable lessons is that you can always get far in life when you have the right people around you. All those who have built something special or remarkable did so by building winning teams. For example, the former Apple CEO, Steve Jobs, built one of the strongest comparison companies in the world, and he attributes his company's amazing success to the power of teams. He emphasized that "great things in business are never done by one person; they're done by a team of people." As in business, so in life, you need to build the right team around you to rocket fuel your success.

The Power of Leverage

Leverage is the ability to use a small amount of resources to achieve a much greater outcome. The concept of leverage is often used in finance and business, where a small investment can be leveraged through borrowing to produce a much larger return. However, leverage can also be applied to other areas of life, such as education, relationships, and personal growth. By investing time, effort, or resources strategically, you can leverage that investment to produce a much larger return. Leverage is one of the main reasons property entrepreneurs are so passionate about the benefits of investing this way. When you make a down payment as a deposit for a property, you can own and control an asset worth many times more than your deposit and reap all the benefits that bring in terms of capital growth and rental income.

The concept of leverage can be applied to studying, just as it can to building a property portfolio. As with real estate, you can invest in focused study and time and then leverage that investment to achieve a much larger result. Here are some strategies for maximizing your time and effort to achieve academic success by assembling a winning team:

- Build a study group. Studying with others is a great way to leverage your study time and effort. Sometimes it's hard to study and grasp concepts alone; therefore, you need to create a team with other students who share the same academic goal so that you can help each other improve and achieve your goals. When you work with others, you learn from their strengths and weaknesses and share ideas and resources to achieve greater success.

- Seek out a mentor: A mentor can be a valuable resource for leveraging your study time and effort. When you work with someone with experience in your field of study, you can gain valuable insights and advice to help you achieve your academic goals. A mentor can also provide motivation and accountability, helping you stay on track and focused on your studies.

- Utilize academic resources: Your school likely offers a range of academic resources, such as tutoring, writing centers, and study groups. Utilizing these resources allows you to gain additional support and guidance in your studies by utilizing these resources. This can assist you in overcoming any academic difficulties you may be experiencing and achieving greater success in your coursework. They'll also have valuable insights into what exam boards are looking for, how to answer certain questions, and how to avoid common mistakes they've seen other students make.

- Make a study schedule: A study schedule can be an extremely effective tool for maximizing your study time and effort. Setting aside dedicated study time allows you to make the most of your study time. Furthermore, by breaking your studies down into manageable chunks, you can make your coursework feel less overwhelming.

- Seek feedback: Getting feedback on your academic performance is critical. You can gain valuable insights into your strengths and weaknesses by soliciting feedback from teachers, classmates, and others. This can assist you in making improvements and achieving greater success in your coursework.

So, if you're looking for ways to succeed, you need to build a winning team. Remember to leverage the power of teamwork and collaboration to achieve your goals. With focus, dedication, and the right strategies, you can achieve academic success and build a bright future.

Teachers and School Time

In your academic journey, teachers will always be one of the primary determinants of who you turn out to be. They directly impact what information you get; they can guide you on how to utilize it to achieve better grades. If you see some of your teachers as a negative force meant to bore you during class sessions, stop and step back. This negative attitude will mean you'll miss out on the benefits of a good student-teacher relationship. I've lost count of the times I've spoken with teacher friends who have tales of children daydreaming, not paying attention, not engaging in class, and then those same students coming unstuck in exams. Try and devour your lessons; learn all you can in the time you have in the classroom. Think of it this way: the more you learn in the classroom, the less time you'll need to study outside of the classroom, and the more time you'll have for other fun stuff!

Establishing a good student-teacher relationship makes you more likely to be engaged and motivated in class. This can lead to better learning outcomes, as you're more likely to pay attention, participate in discussions, and ask questions. When engaged and motivated, you're more likely to remember what you have learned, apply it to new situations, and retain that knowledge for the long term.

You're more likely to receive personalized attention and support when you have a good relationship with your teachers. Teachers who know their students well can identify their strengths and weaknesses and tailor their teaching strategies accordingly. This can help you understand a particular topic or concept, as teachers can provide extra guidance and support to help you catch up.

Additionally, a good student-teacher relationship can lead to better communication between students and teachers. When students feel comfortable talking to their teachers, they are more likely to ask for help when needed and share their concerns or ideas with them. This can help teachers identify areas where students need additional support, leading to a more collaborative and effective learning environment.

Finally, a good student-teacher relationship can help create a positive and supportive learning environment. When you feel valued and respected by your teachers, you will feel positive about yourself and your abilities. This can lead to increased self-esteem and confidence, which can, in turn, lead to better performance in school.

So, how do you develop this positive teacher-student relationship if it doesn't already exist? Three tips to get you started, and remember, this stuff is like a snowball going down a hill; it starts small, but if you just keep going, the impact will be huge:

- **Positive attitude**: consciously make a decision to see your teachers as an amazing resource that you can use to help you achieve the success you're looking for, and in that spirit, listen, engage, and ask questions in class. You have to be in these lessons for this time, so why not make the most of it?

- **Be proactive**: ask questions; seek help. Most teachers want to help, which may sound obvious, but they can't help if you don't put your head above the parapet and ask for it. A 5-minute conversation after class can save you hours of trying to work through a problem at home and all the stress and time-wasting that brings.

- **Seek out allies**: Ok, so you may not get on with the style of your math/Spanish/English teacher, but perhaps there's a teacher you DO engage with who runs the math clinic, the Spanish language club, or the drama society. Find people who you know instinctively will be able to help you, and consciously find ways of learning from them.

Family

This section comes with a massive caveat - most of us have great families, or more likely, great families juggling a gazillion priorities and trying to do their best on all fronts, but not all of us do. If you have a loving, supportive family, then go for it; that's brilliant, and this section has some ideas on how best to work with them so you all come out on top, liking each other more, rather than shouting across the hallway as exam season approaches. But if you don't, and you may not - move on and find value in other sections of this book. For most of us, family wants to support and help us reach our goals. Family can help us engage in that journey. It's also a system and structure that can help us succeed academically.

Your family can be a valuable resource and support system as you work to improve your grades. By involving them strategically and communicating your goals and needs, you can create a winning team around you that helps you achieve academic success. Remember to be open to their ideas and suggestions and to recognize and appreciate their efforts. With a supportive family, you can achieve your academic goals and build a bright future. Here are a couple of ways to benefit from a good family structure:

- Subject-specific assistance: If you're having difficulty with a specific subject, you can ask your family members for assistance. If your parents are good at math, you can ask them to help you with your math homework or to explain difficult concepts. This can also be a great opportunity for bonding and learning from one another. Remember, you're the boss here; it's your success at stake. If the way your dad explains Pythagoras makes no sense, as teaching methods have changed so much since he was at school, let him know that (politely). Perhaps a sibling or an older cousin will be a better choice here.

- Field trips and experiences: Do not roll your eyes when your parents suggest a museum or an exhibition trip. Try to embrace different opportunities, or if it's really not something you want to do, make an effort to suggest an alternative. If walking around the Museum of natural history isn't for you, how about finding an Imax theater with a natural history documentary you can all go to?

- Study assistance: Family members can also assist you with your study habits. You can ask them to assist you in developing a study plan or schedule or to hold you accountable for sticking to it. They can also provide a quiet, distraction-free environment to study in at home.

- Finally, your family can offer emotional support as you navigate the ups and downs of academic life. When you're feeling overwhelmed or stressed, they can provide encouragement, motivation, and perspective and be there when needed. As a child, I always felt too hot in bed the night before important exams. It was always summer (of course), and the evenings were hot and sticky. I found it hard to sleep as I was anxious about the next day. My dad would always come and see me, ask me to hop out of bed, gently and calmly smooth all the bed sheets, and tell me not to worry if I couldn't sleep; that one night of broken sleep wouldn't lead to an exam disaster. I will never forget that calm reassurance expressed through words and actions. If you're fortunate enough to have a parent or carer to provide it, it's food for the soul—enjoy the strength it brings.

It's critical to approach your family with a clear understanding of how they can help you and what you would value from them. You can speak with them and explain your goals and challenges, and ask for their support and feedback. It's also hugely important to acknowledge and appreciate their efforts and contributions and to say thank you. Believe it or not, they will have their own stuff going on, and a bit of appreciation goes a long way.

Friends and Other Students

Your friends should not be people with whom you only hang out, go to parties with, or go on summer trips, but also a group of people willing to help you achieve your goals. You don't have to make friends with people like you, but it's a massive plus to make friends with people who will be your cheerleaders and supporters along the journey and encourage you rather than tell you to just give up. This calls for you to be cautious as you make friends. Making friends with other students with similar interests and academic goals is crucial. Friends will push you to improve by motivating you to study and reminding you about your goals.

When you have friends with the right attitude, you can help each other along by combining study programs, working through problems together, and making studying more fun. And never underestimate the power of networks; your friends expand your network in ways you may never have imagined. They will have their own friends and family who may be able to help. My dad was a whiz at making stuff and helped all my friends with their design technology projects; one of my closest friends' mom was a Spanish teacher who was brilliant at explaining tricky grammar, and so it goes on. The potential is huge.

Friends are also important for emotional support. Sometimes school can be challenging. You may want to give up because of the stressful routines and chunks of assignments that could be overwhelming and exhausting. When you have the right friends around you, they can help elevate your mood and make you realize you're probably not the only one feeling that way.

Furthermore, try to be open to interacting with people who may have interesting perspectives or different skills than you. Your friends may not share similar academic interests; it may well be other students who will be valuable members of your winning team. But please show grace, humility, and respect at all times. If you've been sidelining the class whiz at physics for most of the year because you thought they were dull, don't be surprised when they don't want to help you with a tricky past paper. Behaving like a decent human first is pretty crucial here.

And remember, it goes both ways; your friends and classmates will also be looking for support and help. You can proactively offer to help them with subjects they may find that you've already mastered or to be a study partner for someone struggling to stay organized and focused. If they struggle with creative writing or Spanish, then take the first step and offer to help; you'll probably find the offer is reciprocated—win-win.

Online Resources

In this digital age, there are oodles of online tools and resources available that can help you improve your grades and academic performance. These tools can aid in planning, goal-setting, and studying for exams. Here are some examples of online tools and resources that you can use to boost your academic performance:

- Quizlet: This is a popular app and website that provides flashcards, quizzes, and study games. Quizlet has a vast library of user-generated content that covers almost every subject, making it a great resource for students to use to prepare for exams. Follow this link to access Quizlet: https://quizlet.com/

- Google Drive: This is a cloud-based storage and collaboration platform that allows you to store and share your documents, spreadsheets, and presentations. It also offers features like Google Docs, Sheets, and Slides, which are online versions of Microsoft Office that you can use for free.

- Khan Academy: This website offers free online courses and lessons in various subjects, including mathematics, science, history, and more. The site provides a range of instructional videos, interactive exercises, and assessments that can help you better understand complex concepts.

- Grammarly: This tool can help improve your writing skills by identifying grammatical errors, suggesting vocabulary alternatives, and giving tips on sentence structure and clarity. You can use the free version or upgrade to a paid version for additional features.

- Forest: This app helps you stay focused by planting a digital tree that grows as you avoid using your phone. You can set a timer and work on your assignments without distractions while watching your virtual tree grow.

These are just a few examples of online tools and resources that can help you improve your academic performance. You can find many more by searching or asking your teachers and classmates for recommendations.

For example:

- Ted Talks online/app

- Google art and culture app

- Duolingo app

- Google Scholar

Clubs and Societies

Joining clubs, societies, exhibitions, and shows can be a great way to supplement your learning and improve your grades. These extracurricular activities can expose you to new perspectives, knowledge, and experiences you may not encounter in your regular academic curriculum. Here are some ways you can benefit from these activities:

- **Supplement your learning**: Being part of a club or society related to your academic interests can help you deepen your knowledge and understanding of the subject. You can learn from experts, guest speakers, and fellow members who share your passion. For example, if you're interested in history, joining a historical society can expose you to new research, artifacts, and perspectives that can help you understand the past better. One of the best choices I made in high school was to volunteer to be part of a group working on a diary written by a soldier in the second world war. It turns out he lived near our school and had donated the diary. Visiting and meeting with him gave us all the most amazing perspective on world war II—something we could never have learned from a textbook.

- **Develop new skills**: Clubs and societies can also help you develop new skills that benefit your academic performance. For instance, joining a debate club can help you improve your critical thinking, public speaking, and research skills. These skills can be useful in various subjects, including English, history, and social studies.

- **Make connections**: Joining a club or society can also help you build connections with other students who share your interests and goals. These connections can provide emotional support, study partners, and valuable feedback on your work. You can also learn from each other and collaborate on projects or assignments.

- **Exposure to new experiences**: Attending exhibitions and shows related to your academic interests can help you experience the subject matter in a new way. For instance, visiting a science museum can help you see scientific concepts in action and spark your curiosity for further learning. These experiences can also make your learning more engaging and memorable, making it easier to recall information when it comes time to take a test or write an essay.

So, consider joining one or more of these activities related to your academic interests and see how they can help you improve your grades and overall academic performance. In the next chapter, we'll explore how to pull all of these threads together and how to translate our learning into great notes, powerful essays, and, crucially, how to be effective in exams.

Chapter 8:

How to...

Keep your dreams alive. Understand that to achieve anything requires faith and belief in yourself, vision, hard work, determination, and dedication. Remember, all things are possible for those who believe. –Gail Devers

To succeed in your exams, you need to plan to succeed, work smart, create a winning team, and then be able to make effective notes or study aids so that you can understand and comprehend concepts. Part of winning in high school is writing effective essays and performing well in exams. The good news is that if you've followed all the steps we've talked through already—you'll have a brilliant foundation to springboard into this "delivery phase," when the rewards of all your hard work, strategic thinking, and perseverance will shine through.

Create Effective Notes

Creating effective revision notes is an important aspect of studying for exams and tests. It aids in consolidating your understanding of the subject matter and improving your retention of the information. You must determine which method works best for you to create effective revision notes. Your learning style and personal preferences will influence the method you choose. The most important thing is to write clear, concise, and organized revision notes. Your revision notes should include key concepts, definitions, and examples that you can use to test your comprehension.

Flashcards

Flashcards are a popular method for making revision notes. They are small cards with information, usually in the form of a question and answer. You can use them to assess your understanding of key concepts and definitions. Flashcards are portable and can be used to revise whenever you have a spare moment. This works by using flashcards with a question on one side and an answer on the opposite.

In addition, flashcards can be used to categorize information. You could, for example, make a set of flashcards for each topic and use different colored cards to represent different categories. Flashcards can be used to study with a partner or in a group. Put together your flashcards and quiz each other on the information.

The advantage of using flashcards is that they are portable, so you can carry them anywhere. They are also easy to customize to fit your needs and tailor to your learning style. You can use pictures, words, or diagrams (or a blend of all three), depending on what works best for you.

The downside of flashcards is that they permit limited learning since they are usually brief and do not allow for understanding concepts but rather memorization.

Notes With a Highlighter

Another popular method is to make notes with a highlighter. This entails reviewing your study material and highlighting the key points and important information. You can then create a summary of your notes, highlighting the most important points. This method is effective for visual learners who prefer to see information presented clearly and concisely. You could, for example, use a red highlighter to draw attention to important information or a star symbol to denote key concepts. Remember with this technique that you need active learning, not just underlining. Combine this with some other techniques, such as flashcards or past papers, to ensure you're retaining the knowledge you need and can apply it.

Spidergrams

Spidergrams, also known as mind maps, are a visually organized method of organizing information. They entail creating a diagram that connects various concepts and ideas. This method is ideal for students who prefer a more creative approach to learning and find it easier to remember information when presented visually. Here are some instructions for making spidergrams:

1. Begin with a central concept: Begin by writing your main point in the center of a blank page or by using mind mapping software. This could be a topic or question you want to investigate further.

2. Add subtopics to your spidergram by drawing branches from the center. Each branch should represent a subtopic associated with the main idea. Use keywords and short phrases to describe each subtopic.

3. Connect ideas: Connect related subtopics by drawing lines or branches between them. This will help you see the relationships between ideas and how they are connected.

4. Use colors and images: Use colors and images to make your spidergram more visually appealing and memorable. This can assist you in remembering the information and making it easier to recall later.

5. Review and refine: Once you've finished your spidergram, go over it to make sure it makes sense and that you've included all of the necessary information. Refine the spidergram by adding or removing subtopics as needed.

6. Use Spidergrams to study: Utilize your Spidergram as a study tool by going over it regularly and testing yourself on the information. You can also use your Spidergram to start taking notes or writing essays.

Spidergrams are an effective way to organize and connect information. It's always easier to revise when ideas are connected because it creates a unidirectional flow of information and avoids mixups. They're also great because you can add to them over time as your knowledge of the subject increases, adding in more ideas or connecting different ideas. This is far easier with a spidergram than in linear notes written on a notepad.

Write Powerful Essays That Stand Out

Writing powerful essays is an essential skill you must develop to succeed in your academic career. Writing a powerful essay requires careful planning, research, and effective writing skills, whether for a class assignment, a college application, or a scholarship application. I will discuss five key steps to help you write powerful essays and improve your grades.

Be Crystal Clear About the Purpose of the Essay

Before one word hits the page, you have to have a really clear and compelling story in your head of what this essay is designed to do. Are you composing a descriptive essay about a person, place, or event? Or are you attempting to make an argument or persuade the reader to accept a specific point of view? Without this clarity of purpose, it's all too easy for writing to be vague, inconsistent, loose, and not as powerful as it needs to be.

Thinking about the why before you start also helps shape the content and tone. If it's a descriptive piece, you will want to include creative vocabulary and give space for stories. If it's a piece making an argument in a business or historical context, you will want facts, data, and evidence to back up your points. Thinking about the purpose gets your head in the zone, makes you think about the right areas to focus on, and stops you from heading off in the wrong direction. You don't want to waste time and words creating content that isn't right for the essay. I always find it helpful to write down what you want to accomplish with the essay (on a Post-It on your desk is fine) and loop back to it at various points to ensure I'm on track.

Create an Essay Plan

The next step is to create an essay plan once you've determined what you want to accomplish with your essay. This should be a detailed outline of your essay's sections and structure. An introduction, body paragraphs, and a conclusion should all be included in your essay plan. Each section should be carefully planned and flow logically from one to the next.

Each body paragraph should concentrate on one point or idea related to the topic. Each paragraph should begin with a clear topic sentence that states the paragraph's main idea. You should provide evidence to support your claims and use examples to demonstrate your points.

The conclusion should summarize the essay's key points and restate its purpose. It should also provide a final thought or call to action related to the topic.

Include an Introduction and Conclusion

Make sure to include an introduction and a conclusion in your essay. The introduction should pique the reader's interest while providing background information. It should also clearly state the purpose of the essay and the main points that you will discuss in the essay's body.

The conclusion should summarize the essay's key points and restate its purpose. It should also provide a final thought or call to action related to the topic.

To add to this, you may consider clever use of quotes: Are there quotes from experts or scholars in that field that powerfully put across points? They're a great device, but be careful they are on point and not too long (don't use them to pad essays out).

You may also utilize facts and statistics. However, depending on the essay's purpose, some credible facts and statistics add to your argument. For example, saying millions died in the Second World War is factually accurate, but saying that over 50% of the between 50 and 70 million people who died were civilians tells a compelling story of loss, as does the fact that over 80% of those deaths were from just four countries: Russia, China, and Germany (perhaps not as people would expect).

Create Time to Write and Revise

Creating time to write and revise your essay is an important step in writing. It's important to set aside enough time to write the first draft of your essay, as well as time to revise and edit it.

After completing your first draft, take a break from your essay and return to it later with fresh eyes. This break will provide you with a fresh perspective on your writing and assist you in identifying any areas that require additional revision.

Edit the Draft Before Submission

Before submitting an essay, the final step is to edit the draft. Examine your essay critically and ask yourself if it achieves what you intended. Does the structure work? Are there any clumsy words or sentences that you can edit?

Reading your essay aloud or having someone else read it to you can be beneficial. This will assist you in identifying any awkward or unclear sentences and will help you ensure that your writing flows smoothly.

To summarize, writing good essays is an important skill that high school students must develop to succeed academically. If you follow these five steps, you can write a well-structured, persuasive essay that will help you achieve your academic goals.

Be Effective in Exams

Being effective in exams is an essential skill for high school students who are looking to improve their grades. Effective exam preparation involves a combination of strategies, including time management, careful reading, understanding the question requirements, attempting all questions, and using all the available time. We will discuss the key strategies you can use to be effective in your exams. I mentioned earlier that I used to fear sitting for exams because I was overwhelmed by the fear of failure. However, when I began using the following strategies when taking exams, my grades improved overall.

Remember, if you've put in the thinking, the study, and even some of the strategies we've discussed, here is your chance to shine. Try to approach it that way, even if you feel sick, stressed, and anxious. Take a breath; you can do it.

Plan Your Time

Okay, so this sounds simple, but many students just don't do it. The first step toward exam success is to organize your time. As the invigilator says, "Turn over your paper and begin," your stomach will be somersaulting, and you'll be scanning the paper to see what's in it, which questions are "your questions," and whether you can pull it off. Then take a breath and think about how best to use your time. Remember this, above anything else, allocate your time based on the number of marks for each question.

Importance of Reading the Question

In exams, it's critical to read the question carefully. Read the question for the first time to familiarize yourself with it. Read it a second time to assess what the question demands. Then reread it to ensure you understand what the question requires.

To understand what is being asked, highlight the keywords. Determine whether the question requests a description, explanation, analysis, or evaluation. Once you understand the question, make sure that you answer it according to the requirements. Be crystal clear on the "ask" before you start to answer; it's very easy to describe rather than evaluate, to list rather than explain, or to give examples rather than discuss how the writer achieves this.

Do the Easiest Questions First

Begin with the simplest questions first. This will help you gain confidence and momentum. You will have more time to focus on the more difficult questions later if you finish the easier questions first. In addition, attempting the easiest questions first helps prevent the panic that would arise by starting with the harder ones.

The goal we all aim for when attempting exams is to attain amazing grades, and one way to maximize marks in the exam or test is by starting with questions you're more knowledgeable about and sure about.

Attempt All Questions

It's essential to attempt all questions in an exam. Do not leave any questions unanswered, even if you're unsure. In the case of multiple-choice questions, it's better to guess an answer than leave the question unanswered.

While I was in high school, my teacher always told me to never leave anything unanswered. Even if you have a slight idea, write it down and build around it. He said that if there was a borderline pass and the paper was under review, it would be hard to award marks where the answer booklet was blank.

If You Run Out of Time

Sometimes, it's normal to run out of time even when you plan because there could be much more to write than you thought, or the questions are more taxing than you had imagined. If you run out of time, create bullet points for the remainder of the essay questions. This way, you can be awarded marks for your thinking and reasoning. Even if you do not have time to write complete sentences or paragraphs, ensure your answers are legible and coherent.

Use All the Time

Use all the time available in the exam. Do not look out the window and feel relieved once you've finished the paper. Review your answers, check for errors, and return to the areas you found tricky to see if you can fill in any blanks. The time is there for you to use it, so use it. I had a friend who used to submit her paper when she finished. She never waited for the time allocated for the exam to run out. However, her habit started catching up with her. Her grades started to sink, and the teacher told her that her essays had a lot of errors, many of which were due to question misinterpretation and not a lack of knowledge.

Being effective in your exams is critical to improving your grades. If you implement these strategies consistently and effectively, they will help you improve on exams. And try not to dread exams above anything else; try to look at them as a stepping stone, an opportunity to showcase all your knowledge and skills. You need not look at them as a problem but rather as a step toward the next phase of your life.

In the next chapter, we'll discuss the common challenges and how you can overcome them.

Chapter 9:

Help!

It may sound paradoxical, but strength comes from vulnerability. You have to ask the question to get the answer, even though asking the question means you don't know. –Majid Kazmi

In Chapter 7, we discussed creating a winning team and established that success is not a solo act and that seeking help from others is okay. Sometimes, despite our best efforts, things don't go according to plan, and the pressure may build up as you stress over improving your grades and reading extensively.

Leaving It Late

You may find yourself in a situation where you have left your exam preparation too late or have created an unrealistic revision schedule, resulting in a growing sense of panic. Try not to panic; you can always do things to improve your situation. Here are some strategies for managing your situation and increasing your chances of success.

Take a Breath

The first step is to relax and take a deep breath. When we are overwhelmed, our natural reaction is to panic. However, panicking, while understandable, only makes matters worse, so try to remain calm and composed. Remember that there is no exam that you cannot come back from. Even if things do not go as planned, there are always ways to improve in the future by learning from the experience. Remember this, and try not to make the same mistakes again.

Focus on the Critical

Now is the time to be ruthless with your focus. Identify the critical areas within each subject that you know will be tested. Make a point of prioritizing these areas and allocating your time and energy accordingly. Focus on the must-have topics, not the nice-to-have ones. This way, you can maximize your chances of scoring well on the exam.

Reach Out for Help

Don't be afraid to ask your teachers or classmates for assistance. Teachers can advise you on which topics to prioritize and which materials to study. They may also be able to recommend additional resources or provide additional assistance to assist you in catching up. Your classmates may also have useful insights and tips for exam preparation.

Eat Well and Rest Up

While it may be tempting to reach for the chocolate and stay up late studying, it's critical to prioritize your physical and mental health while preparing for exams. Eat healthy, well-balanced meals, and get plenty of rest. Aim for seven to eight hours of sleep per night to keep your mind and body fresh and alert for the exam.

Always Have a Go

Finally, it's critical to maintain a positive attitude and not give up before you have even begun. Even if you feel unprepared, you should always attempt the exam. Keep in mind that the worst that can happen is that you fail. However, if you do not take the exam, you will not be able to benefit from the experience. Believe in yourself; you might be surprised at how much you know.

If you have left your exam preparation too late or created an unrealistic revision timetable, there are always things you can do to improve your situation. With the steps outlined above, you can increase your chances of success while also learning from the experience.

You Just Don't Get It

I understand how frustrating it can be to work hard to improve your grades only to feel as if you just don't understand it. You may feel as if you're not making any progress despite trying different approaches. However, I want to assure you there will be a way through.

First and foremost, remember not to regard yourself as stupid or incapable. These negative thoughts will only serve to hold you back. Instead, try to adopt a growth mindset. Recognize this is a challenge, and you can overcome it. You just need to find a different approach.

One thing you can do is return to your learning style. Are you leveraging the way you learn best for this particular problem? If you're a visual learner, try making diagrams or mind maps to help you understand the material better. If you're an auditory learner, record yourself reciting important information and listen to it repeatedly.

Another strategy you can employ is to return to your superpower. What are you naturally good at? What strategies can you employ to capitalize on your strengths? If you're a creative writer, try writing a story or poem incorporating the concepts you're struggling with.

If you've tried everything and still aren't seeing results, it's time to try something new. As Winnie the Pooh once said, "The definition of insanity is doing the same thing over and over and expecting a different result" (Quote Investigator, 2017, para. 1). Try something different if you've tried studying from your notes, watching videos, and attending classes. For example, form a study group with classmates, ask your teacher for extra help, or try a different textbook or online resource.

Remember that improving your grades is a journey; seeing the desired results may take time and effort to see the desired results. But don't give up hope. Continue experimenting with different strategies until you find the one that works best.

Stressed and Overwhelmed

It can get overwhelming and stressful when trying to improve your grades, and it seems like nothing is working. In moments like these, it's important to take a step back, give yourself space to breathe and reset.

It's critical to remember that feeling stressed and overwhelmed is completely normal. Everyone has these feelings at some point, and you will feel them again. Don't berate yourself for it. Instead, try one or more of these strategies until you feel more at ease. Trust me; they do work.

One effective strategy is to take a break. Put down your pens, leave your desk, and get outside. Go for a walk in the fresh air. Spending time in nature can have a calming effect on the mind and reduce stress levels.

Another excellent strategy is to do something enjoyable. This could include anything from catching up with friends to spending time with your pet dog or watching a favorite movie. Doing things that make you happy can help you divert your attention away from stress and provide you with a much-needed mental break.

Breathing exercises are another effective stress-reduction technique. Try deep breathing exercises such as box breathing. Box breathing is a simple technique that involves taking slow, deep breaths in a structured pattern. It's commonly used as a relaxation and stress-reducing technique, helping to calm the mind and body.

The concept of box breathing is derived from creating a square shape with your breath, where each side of the square represents a specific phase of the breathing pattern. Here's how it typically works:

1. Find a comfortable sitting or lying position. Close your eyes if it helps you focus.

2. Begin by exhaling completely, emptying your lungs as much as possible.

3. Inhale slowly and deeply through your nose, counting to a specific number, such as four.

4. Once you have taken a full breath in, hold your breath for the same count, maintaining a comfortable and relaxed state.

5. Exhale slowly and fully through your mouth, again counting to the same number.

6. Hold your breath for the same count before starting the cycle again.

The key to box breathing is to keep each breath phase equal in duration: inhaling, holding, exhaling, and holding again. The specific count can vary depending on personal preference or guidance, but consistency is essential throughout the practice.

Deeply inhale, hold for a few seconds, and slowly exhale. Repeat this a few times, and you'll feel your body relax.

Try to keep perspective; this is hard; I appreciate it. Passing that exam or getting into that college may well be the biggest or most important hurdle life throws at you. Focus on the fact that you're bigger and more important than any exam or qualification; you will still be you regardless; your friends and family will still love you, and regardless of the outcome, there will be a good path forward.

Finally, be gentle with yourself. We are all our harshest critics, but it's important to listen to that inner voice and ask yourself, "Would I say that to a friend in my shoes?" The answer is most likely no. Consider what you would say to a friend and apply that same kindness to yourself. Most likely, it would be something like, "You're fantastic. Everyone feels this way. How can I help?"

Remember that while improving your grades is important, your mental health and well-being should always come first. Don't forget to take care of yourself and use these stress-management strategies when things get tough.

Regroup

Now that you've de-stressed and reset, it's time to regroup and determine where you are and where you need to go from here. This is important in improving your grades and reaching your academic objectives.

- Begin by assessing where you are in your studies right now. Examine your grades and any feedback you've received from teachers or professors. This will give you a good idea of where you stand and where to concentrate your efforts.

- Next, re-plan your approach. If what you've been doing hasn't been working, it's time to try something new. Consider your learning style and consider what strategies might work best for you. Maybe you're a visual learner and need to use more diagrams and mind maps to help you remember information. Or perhaps you're an auditory learner and need to record yourself reading your notes and listening to them while you study.

- It's also essential to set realistic goals for yourself. Don't try to do too much at once, as this can quickly become overwhelming. Instead, break down your goals into manageable tasks and work on them individually. This will help you stay focused and motivated.

- Remember to take deep breaths and stay calm when things get tough. Getting caught up in the stress and pressure of trying to improve your grades is easy, but taking a step back and looking at things objectively can help you maintain a clear head.

- Don't be afraid to ask for help. Reach out to teachers, professors, or tutors if you're struggling with a particular subject. They can offer guidance and support to help you overcome any obstacles.

- It's also important to take care of yourself outside of school. Make time for hobbies and activities you enjoy, and prioritize self-care activities such as exercise, meditation, and getting enough sleep. A healthy mind and body are crucial for academic success.

- Finally, remember that success is not just about grades. It's about learning and growing as a person. Don't get too caught up in the numbers, and remember that every experience, whether a success or a failure, is an opportunity to learn and improve.

To summarize, improving your grades can be difficult and sometimes overwhelming, but it's doable with the right mindset and strategies. Take some time to reflect, re-plan, and stay focused on your objectives. Don't be afraid to ask for help and prioritize your own well-being. Remember that success is more than just grades; it's also about personal growth and learning. You've got this.

In the next chapter, we will talk about the D-day—the exam day.

Chapter 10:

Today Is the Day

Education's purpose is to replace an empty mind with an open one. –Malcolm
Forbes

The exam day is a special one. It's meant to sum up all your efforts into
one or two hours. The day comes with some tension and anxiety. It
demands that you block out everything that may affect your success and
channel all your focus to this particular moment. In this chapter, we'll
explore the dos and don'ts of exam day.

The Dos

It's critical to double-check your equipment before leaving for the exam.
Nothing is more frustrating than discovering that you're missing
something during an exam. Check that you have the proper pens, a ruler,
a calculator, and any other math equipment you may need. Check with
your teacher or exam guidelines to see what is permitted, and ensure you
have everything on the list. Remember that you will be under stress
during the exam, so having everything you need on hand will help you
focus and avoid unnecessary stress. Bring some spares! A couple of spare
pens, pencils, and rubber—it all helps ease nerves and prevent last-
minute hitches.

Getting an early night is essential for your mental and physical well-being
on the exam day. Many students believe cramming the night before is a
good idea, but in reality, pulling an all-nighter is a misconception. Pulling

an all-nighter will only leave you feeling exhausted and unprepared for the exam. Instead, aim to get at least seven to eight hours of sleep the night before the exam. This will help you stay focused during the exam and feel more alert and energized. If you're having trouble sleeping because of nerves or stress, try relaxation techniques like deep breathing or meditation.

Consuming a nutritious breakfast on the day of the exam is critical. Breakfast is the most important meal of the day, and this is especially true on exam day. A nutritious breakfast will give you the energy to remain focused and alert during the exam. Choose a meal that balances blood sugar levels, and avoid sugary cereals or pastries that will cause a sugar crash later in the day. Instead, choose high-protein foods like eggs, low-sugar granola, or cereal to keep you full and energized for longer.

Going in with a positive mindset is crucial. Your attitude toward the exam can have a big impact on how well you do. If you approach the situation with a negative mindset, you may experience anxiety, stress, or overwhelm, impairing your ability to concentrate and recall information. It's essential to approach the exam with a positive mindset. Believe in yourself and your abilities, and trust that you have prepared well. Maintain your focus on the task at hand and avoid being distracted by negative thoughts. Remember that maintaining a positive attitude can help you stay calm, focused, and motivated during the exam.

Dial in all the learnings from Chapter 8 about being effective in exams. Understanding exam technique is just as important as revising content. Therefore, make sure to read through all the points in Chapter 8 carefully and make a note of the key exam techniques. Plan your time and allocate it to each section according to its importance. Keep an eye on the clock during the exam, and stick to your allocated time. By doing so, you can avoid wasting time on one section and leaving another section incomplete.

Reading the question thoroughly is an important exam technique. Highlight the keywords and determine whether the question asks what, how, or when. This will help you understand the question better and avoid answering the incorrect question. Make sure to read the instructions and questions carefully and to answer all parts of the question. Instead of assuming what the examiner wants, stick to what the question asks you to do.

Make an effort to answer all questions, especially multiple-choice questions. Many students avoid questions that they find difficult or time-consuming, but this is a mistake. Even if you don't get all of the questions right, answering them all will earn you points. When answering multiple-choice questions, carefully read all of the options and eliminate those you know are incorrect. Make an educated guess based on your knowledge of the subject if you're unsure. Remember, every mark counts, and you never know which question might be the one that tips the scales in your favor.

An essential exam-day hack is to do the easiest questions first. This is an effective exam strategy that can help you gain momentum and confidence at the start of the exam. By tackling the easier questions first, you can avoid getting stuck and losing confidence early on in the exam. Additionally, completing the easier questions can help you allocate more time to the more challenging questions later in the exam.

Create bullet points for the remaining essay questions if you run out of time. This is a useful technique for essay-based exams where you may not have enough time to complete all the questions. In this scenario, creating bullet points for the remaining questions is better than leaving them blank. Doing this allows you to demonstrate your knowledge and understanding of the topic and gain marks for your thinking and reasoning.

Use all the time provided. It can be tempting to rush through the exam and feel relieved once you've finished the paper. However, this can be a mistake. You should take the time to read through the exam carefully, check for errors, and return to any areas you found tricky to see if you can fill in any blanks. The time provided in the exam is there for you to use, so make the most of it.

Checking for errors is an important part of the exam. It's common to make mistakes in the heat of the moment, and checking for errors can help you catch any errors you may have missed. Check your calculations, spelling, and grammar carefully. In essay-based exams, ensure your arguments are logical and well-supported, and check for any unclear or incomplete sentences. You can avoid losing marks for careless errors by taking the time to check for them.

The Don'ts

Avoid using social media in the run-up to exams. Regarding exam preparation, social media can be a double-edged sword. On the one hand, it can be a valuable resource for locating study materials and connecting with other students. On the other hand, social media can be a major source of distraction and anxiety, especially during exam season. People on social media tend to present only their best selves, which can create unrealistic expectations and make you feel bad about yourself. Avoid using social media during exam times and concentrate on your preparation.

Do not—I repeat, do not—discuss how much revision your friends have done outside the exam hall. It's tempting to compare yourself to others and see how much revision your friends have completed. This, however, can lead to unnecessary stress and anxiety. Everyone revises at their own pace and in their own way, so comparing yourself to others is pointless. Concentrate on your own preparation and have faith that you have done enough to perform well on the exam. Many times, it's those who shout the loudest who have the least to say. Several times, I've heard stories from teachers about students proudly boasting about how much revision they've done just before an exam, who then go on to do a moderate performance. In contrast, many others, who were far more discreet and quietly went about the business at hand, performed far more strongly. Remember: Swim in your lane and try to block out the noise of others.

Try not to replay the exam over and over again. Reflecting on how you performed and what you could have done better after an exam is natural. However, it's critical to strike a balance between reflection and progress. Reliving the exam can cause unnecessary stress and anxiety, preventing you from focusing on the next exam. When the exam is finished, focus on the next one and wait for the results.

Don't measure yourself against others. It's just as important to avoid social media as it is to avoid comparing yourself to your classmates or friends before or after the exam. Everyone has different strengths and weaknesses and approaches studying and exams differently. Don't be concerned with what others are doing; concentrate on your performance.

Don't panic if you don't know the answer. During an exam, it's normal to come across a question to which you do not know the answer. Instead of panicking, take a deep breath and proceed to the next question. Don't let what you cannot do interfere with what you can do. You can always return to the difficult questions later. Remember that it's preferable to attempt all of the questions, even if you're unsure of the answer, rather than leaving them blank.

Don't rush through the exam. While time management is essential during an exam, rushing through the questions can lead to careless errors. Take your time reading the questions and understanding what is being asked. Plan your time wisely, and if you find yourself short on time, use bullets to jot down your thoughts and ideas quickly.

Don't cram at the last minute. Many students believe they can cram all the information they need right before the exam. However, this is not an effective study technique and can be detrimental to your performance. Instead, in the days leading up to the exam, try to review your notes and practice previous exam questions. You'll be able to enter the exam with a clear mind and a solid understanding of the material if you do this.

Going into an exam is far from easy. The most important thing is that you're prepared for the exam; all you need to do is calm down, relax, and be optimistic. In the last chapter, we will explore what happens when you're done writing the exam.

Chapter 11:

And Breathe

I do not try to dance better than anyone else. I only try to dance better than myself. —
Arianna Huffington

Everyone fails at some stage—at an exam, in a relationship, in a job—
and when it happens to you, it's hard, but you can come back from it.
Failure after putting in all the effort is the ultimate test of resilience and
patience. Here are some thoughts on how to deal with it:

Thought or Reality

Did you fail, or do you think you failed? It's important to establish if you
failed, not just a feeling or thought. Well, if it's just a thought, hold your
horses—the world is full of people who thought they had flunked an
exam when they had not failed.

Usually, we second-guess the answers we wrote in the exam, making us
think we failed. Additionally, when we interact with our friends with
whom we answered the same exam, they make us rethink our answers,
raising thoughts of failure.

When I was a student, whenever we finished answering our exams, we
would hang around in the corridor and discuss the questions to assess if
we had passed. It was a very common thing most of us took part in.
After the discussion, some of us felt worried because our answers
contrasted with those of other students, whom we thought were brighter
than us. This made us feel low and ruined our moods. The next few

weeks until the exam release always felt like hell. It was hard to go through them with all the anxiety and tension. I always wondered how I would explain to my parents that I had failed and how my peers would look at me. It was hard being in that position. Surprisingly, when the results were returned, I had passed, and those we thought had passed with flying colors had maybe not done as well as we had imagined. I'm not saying it was like that all the time, but on several occasions, it turned out just like that. Of course, I would be thrilled, but then I would wonder why I was so sickly worried in the first place.

While discussing the dos and don'ts, we agreed that we should not engage in post-exam discussions with other students after the exam because we bring stress and anxiety to ourselves. The best way to find out if you have passed or failed is simply to wait for the results; they are the only way to confirm where you are. After finding out where you stand, you get to decide what to do next.

What Next

If you really have flunked the exam and missed the mark, you need to compose yourself and not beat yourself up. It's understandable to feel disappointed and frustrated if you know you've performed poorly on an exam. However, it's important not to let these negative thoughts spiral out of control and affect your self-esteem and confidence. Remember, everyone experiences failure in life—not once but many times. They may not shout about it, but they will have experienced it. Remember this quote from Winston Churchill, a man who experienced many setbacks in his life as well as many triumphs: "Success is not final; failure is not fatal; it is the courage to continue that counts." This quote speaks to the transitory nature of both success and failure and the importance of perseverance.

Acknowledge your emotions and give yourself space to process them. Allow yourself to feel disappointed, frustrated, or upset, but try not to dwell on these emotions for too long. Instead, use them as motivation to improve and do better in the future.

Remember that one exam does not define your entire academic career or your future success. While grades are important, they are not the only measure of intelligence or potential. History is littered with successful and accomplished people who had to overcome failure and challenges on their path to success. Look at Albert Einstein; his teacher told him he would never make it because he could not grasp concepts and failed exams. Years later, he became one of the greatest physicists of all time.

It's critical to step back and evaluate the situation objectively. Try to figure out what went wrong and what you could do differently next time. Did I not study enough? Did I misunderstand the material? Did I not manage my time effectively during the exam? Identifying these factors can help you develop a plan to improve.

Explore your options and make the best decision. This might include retaking the exam during the summer so your schedule does not change. Additionally, you can take a summer course to improve your knowledge and skills or consider a slightly different next step or course. You can discuss these options with your school counselor or academic advisor, who can provide you with more information about each option and help you decide what's best for you.

During this time, you need to seek help if you need it. Speak with your teacher or a tutor to identify areas for additional assistance. They may be able to provide additional resources and strategies to help you better understand the material and prepare for future exams.

Look after yourself; maintain your physical health. Maintain your physical health by getting enough sleep, eating well, and exercising regularly. Take care of your mental health by doing things you enjoy that help you relax and de-stress.

Finally, it's important to remember that setbacks are a natural part of life. As hard as it may be, you need to look at the situation through a positive lens. More than ever, you need your growth mindset to establish that you can bounce back stronger regardless of the results. There are very few things in life that you can't come back from, and even failures can provide valuable learning opportunities. Use this setback to reflect on your goals and aspirations and devise a strategy to achieve them. Spielberg, one of the most successful directors in cinema history, was rejected from film school several times and struggled in his early career. He persisted, however, and went on to direct some of the most iconic films of all time.

Michael Jordan, widely regarded as one of the greatest basketball players of all time, was cut from his high school basketball team as a sophomore. However, he used this setback as motivation to work harder, and he went on to have an extremely successful career, winning numerous awards and accolades. Oprah Winfrey, reflecting on being fired from her first TV job, went on to say, "There's no such thing as failure; failure is just life trying to push us in another direction.

Conclusion

All our dreams come true if we have the courage to pursue them. –Walt Disney

Like many ultimately successful people, Walt Disney faced many challenges on his road to success. He faced multiple setbacks that would have easily made him give up on his goals, but he did not. Amidst several debts and failed projects, he still held the courage to continue on his journey. His film career met with a lot of opposition, even after he produced Mickey Mouse, which was a success. Disney continued to pursue his dream. As a film producer, he still holds the record for most Academy Awards earned and nominations for an individual, having won 22 Oscars from 59 nominations. Films such as The Jungle Book, Sleeping Beauty, and Mary Poppins are still incredibly popular decades later, and Disneyland theme parks continue to attract millions of visitors a year (Pak, 2020).

As a teenager struggling to improve your grades, there are lots of lessons to learn from Walt Disney and others who have achieved despite facing challenges along the way. These lessons are the strategies detailed in this book—strategies you can incorporate into your everyday life to improve your habits and become more successful in life.

In Chapter 1, I discussed the concept of your superpower, and the key takeaway was to understand the importance of your superpower and how to identify it. It's through understanding what you're good at that you can leverage it to further your success and boost your self-esteem and confidence.

In Chapter 2, I emphasized the benefits of finding your "why" in life. You get to attach purpose to your life and also learn how to develop important skills that you can utilize to improve your grades. The most important aspect of this chapter is understanding how to set SMART goals. Your goals to succeed should be specific, measurable, achievable, relevant, and time-bound.

Another interesting concept I covered is the growth mindset. In Chapter 3, I discuss the importance of having a growth mindset. It's important that you look at the challenges in your academic journey as opportunities to develop new skills or try new approaches and appreciate the power of "yet." We may not be good at that particular subject "yet," but change is absolutely possible.

In the following chapter, I discussed the different learning styles. Are you a visual or auditory learner? I provided tips on how you can identify your learning style so that you can integrate strategies that will help you get the most out of your particular learning style.

In Chapter 5, the focus was on planning to succeed. I discussed the benefits of planning your academic journey and also put emphasis on how you can plan. On your academic journey, you need to have a plan on how to achieve your goals, and in this chapter, we explored the best ways to achieve them.

In chapter 6 we looked at how smart works beats hard work because who wants to spend all 24 hours studying and cramming concepts when they can focus on their "why," eat the frog, or utilize the miracle morning technique to achieve their grades with a little more ease?

In Chapter 7, I ensured that we understood the importance of teamwork and how you can create a winning team. You're not competing against your fellow students, but your fight is against poor grades, and you need to have your teachers, friends, family and other students on your team to help you achieve the grades you aspire for.

Success does not come to you just because you want it; you need to put in the effort by creating effective notes, writing good essays, and ensuring you're effective in exams. In Chapter 8, I discuss different ways you can do all that.

In Chapter 9, I discussed ways to manage the pressure from common problems, such as leaving revision until the last minute and being unable to grasp certain subjects. In this chapter, I encouraged you to seek help if you need it. You need to take it easy on yourself because you're only human, and sometimes things just don't work out as you would have wished and planned.

On exam day, there are things you need to do and things you do not need to do because they directly affect how you will perform. You need to eat well, sleep enough, go in with a positive mindset, and check if you have all the equipment you need for that exam. In Chapter 10, I also emphasized that you need to avoid social media before and after your exam and not replay the exam in your head once it's done.

In our final chapter, I addressed how to deal with failure if it happens. It's part of life. We have all failed at some point; we may still fail at a future stage in life. Self-pity and criticism may be necessary, but you do not have to dwell on the failure but rather seek ways to overcome it. If you have failed your math exam, you need to find out why you failed and then find ways to improve. It's essential to develop a working relationship with your teachers so that they can advise you accordingly.

History is littered with amazing, accomplished people who have succeeded despite facing obstacles. For example, Sylvester Stallone, one of the most famous actors of this generation, has one of the most inspiring stories ever. Before he became a famous actor, he could barely foot his bills or even afford all his meals in a day. His struggles with life hit rock bottom when he had to sell his dog to make a living. He did not give up, enduring the lows. He kept searching, enduring, and keeping a positive mindset (Team, 2022). After several years of acting in insignificant roles in different movies, he finally broke through, and since that moment, his life has never been the same. Sylvester is just one of the many people who have managed to make it out of hard situations, and you, too, can. Your story may not be as similar or as hard as his, but you're fighting your own battle, and this book is designed to give you a whole smorgasbord of tactics to win your way through.

I hope you've found this book useful and that it's given you lots of ideas, tools, and techniques to help you improve how you study and how you feel about studying and why you're doing it. It's a book to revisit and come back to when you have specific challenges. I hope you'll always find something new to try or a fresh take on what you're doing.

Remember, keep going; don't give up. If something isn't working, take a look and try some new techniques and approaches. I leave you with the inspiring words of Hal Elrod, author of *Miracle Morning*: "When you consistently maintain unwavering faith and put forth an extraordinary effort over an extended period of time, you cannot fail. You may stumble and experience setbacks, but your success will ultimately move from possible to probable to inevitable" (Elrod, 2017).

Thank you for reading! If you enjoyed this book, we'd really appreciate it if you could leave a review on Amazon. This will help us continue to provide great books, and it will help our potential buyers make confident buying decisions. We'd be forever grateful – thank you in advance!

References

Asking For Help Quotes. (n.d.). *Goodreads*. Www.goodreads.com. https://www.goodreads.com/quotes/tag/asking-for-help

A quote by Henry Ford. (2019). *Goodreads*. Goodreads.com. https://www.goodreads.com/quotes/978-whether-you-think-you-can-or-you-think-you-can-t--you-re

A quote by Meryl Streep. (n.d.). *Goodreads*. Www.goodreads.com. https://www.goodreads.com/quotes/9918565-what-makes-you-different-or-weird-that-s-your-strength

A quote by Walt Disney Company. (n.d.). *Goodreads*. Www.goodreads.com. https://www.goodreads.com/quotes/1283-all-our-dreams-can-come-true-if-we-have-the

Az Quotes. (n.d.). *Jennifer Lopez Quote*. A-Z Quotes. Retrieved May 10, 2023, from https://www.azquotes.com/quote/823655

Be strong, be fearless, be beautiful. And believe that anything is possible when you have the right people there to support you. - Misty Copeland - Quotespedia.org. (n.d.). *quotespedia.org*. Www.quotespedia.org. Retrieved May 10, 2023, from https://www.quotespedia.org/authors/m/misty-copeland/be-strong-be-fearless-be-beautiful-and-believe-that-anything-is-possible-when-you-have-the-right-people-there-to-support-you-misty-copeland/

Bhatt, P. (2022, February 21). *5 Famous Visual-Spatial Learners In The History*. Number Dyslexia. https://numberdyslexia.com/famous-visual-spatial-learners/

Bokhari, D. (2020, May 25). *Marginal Gains: Transform Your Life by Getting 1% Better Each Day*. Dean Bokhari. https://www.deanbokhari.com/marginal-gains/

Chilton, L. (2021, March 7). *A timeline of Oprah Winfrey's career*. The Independent. https://www.independent.co.uk/arts-entertainment/tv/news/oprah-winfrey-career-timeline-harry-meghan-b1813630.html

Community, S. (2022, June 1). *55+ Inspirational School Quotes for Every Student | Shutterfly*. Ideas & Inspiration. https://www.shutterfly.com/ideas/school-quotes/?CID=SEGOO.OTHER.21700000001930203_717000 00092514532_58700007760053814&&CID=SEGOO.OTHER .387_338509_8345552_dsa&gclid=Cj0KCQjwgLOiBhC7ARIs AIeetVD2_0krI5CdleyeANFhdxm5w2_2sMxxSCn3HkUNSxg A4z53McJgO0saAgeLEALw_wcB&gclsrc=aw.ds

Dweck, C. S. (2006). *Mindset: the New Psychology of Success*. Random House.

Earl Nightingale Quotes. (n.d.). *BrainyQuote*. BrainyQuote. https://www.brainyquote.com/quotes/earl_nightingale_15904 4

Edinburgh, K.-A. (2021, April 1). *49 Inspirational Exam Quotes For Students: Ultimate Motivation*. Exam Study Expert. https://examstudyexpert.com/inspirational-exam-quotes/

Elrod, H. (2017). *The Miracle Morning : The Not-So-Obvious Secret Guaranteed To Transform Your Life Before 8 Am*. Hal Elrod International, Inc.

Feddes, J. (2013, February 28). *20 Must-See TED talks for Planning Professionals*. Plan Academy. https://www.planacademy.com/20-must-see-ted-talks-planning-professionals/

Gallup Inc. (n.d.). *StrengthsFinder 2.0*. Gallup.com. https://www.gallup.com/cliftonstrengths/en/strengthsfinder.a spx

Guasch-Ferré, M., & Willett, W. C. (2021). The Mediterranean diet and health: a comprehensive overview. *Journal of Internal Medicine, 290*(3), 549–566. https://doi.org/10.1111/joim.13333

Horan, K. S. (2021, September 29). *10 Signs of a Problem with Perfectionism | Psychology Today.* Www.psychologytoday.com. https://www.psychologytoday.com/us/blog/the-reality-gen-z/202109/10-signs-problem-perfectionism

Jay. (2022, March 18). *10 Famous people with a growth mindset.* Mind by Design. https://www.mindbydesign.io/famous-people-with-a-growth-mindset/#:~:text=10%20Famous%20people%20with%20a%20growth%20mindset%201

May, E. (2020). *20 Quotes That Will Inspire You to Work Smarter, Not Harder.* Www.niagarainstitute.com. https://www.niagarainstitute.com/blog/work-smarter-not-harder-quotes

Mehta, K. (2021, March 10). *A Harvard psychologist says humans have 8 types of intelligence. Which ones do you score the highest in?* CNBC. https://www.cnbc.com/2021/03/10/harvard-psychologist-types-of-intelligence-where-do-you-score-highest-in.html

Mind. (2022, August). *About self-esteem.* Mind.org.uk. https://www.mind.org.uk/information-support/types-of-mental-health-problems/self-esteem/about-self-esteem/

Never Give Up Quotes. (n.d.). *Goodreads* . Www.goodreads.com. https://www.goodreads.com/quotes/tag/never-give-up

Norris, E. (2019, March 19). *30 inspiring quotes for your students*. Learn; Canva. https://www.canva.com/learn/30-inspiring-quotes-students/

Obama, B. (2020). *A promised land*. Crown Publishing Group.

Pak, E. (2020, June 17). *Walt Disney's Rocky Road to Success*. Biography. https://www.biography.com/movies-tv/walt-disney-failures

Pinterest. (n.d.). *Pin on Inspirational Quotes*. Pinterest. Retrieved May 11, 2023, from https://www.pinterest.com/pin/301319031303773247/#:~:text=Inspirational%20Quote-%20%22Every%20child%20has%20a%20different%20learning

Popik, B. (n.d.). *Barry Popik*. Www.barrypopik.com. Retrieved May 10, 2023, from https://www.barrypopik.com/index.php/new_york_city/entry/be_sure_you_put_your_feet_in_the_right_place_then_stand_firm#:~:text=Lincoln%20was%20helping%20Rebecca%20R.%20Pomeroy%20%281817-1884%29%2C%20an

Quote Investigator. (2017, March 24). *Insanity Is Doing the Same Thing Over and Over Again and Expecting Different Results – Quote Investigator*. Quoteinvestigator.com. https://quoteinvestigator.com/2017/03/23/same/

Scroggs, L. (2022). *The Pomodoro Technique – Why It Works & How To Do It*. Todoist. https://todoist.com/productivity-methods/pomodoro-technique

Talerico, A. (2022, November 24). *SMART Goals*. Corporate Finance Institute. https://corporatefinanceinstitute.com/resources/management/smart-goal/

Taube, A. (2014, September). *What 11 Extremely Successful People Learned From Failure.* Business Insider. https://www.businessinsider.com/what-successful-people-learned-from-failure-2014-9?r=US&IR=T#mark-cuban-learned-he-only-had-to-be-right-once-2

Team, T. S. (2022, February 3). *TOP 10 INSPIRATIONAL SUCCESS STORIES TO KEEP YOU STRIVING FOR YOUR DREAMS.* The STRIVE. https://thestrive.co/inspirational-success-stories/

Tracy, B. (2013). Eat That Frog!: Get More Of The Important Things Done Today. In *Amazon.* Hodder Paperbacks. https://www.amazon.co.uk/Eat-That-Frog-Important-Things/dp/1444765426/ref=sr_1_1?crid=2BQZ9LT74T4I6&keywords=eat+the+frog&qid=1684251236&sprefix=eat+the+frog%2Caps%2C95&sr=8-1

Made in the USA
Las Vegas, NV
05 July 2024

91874697R00075